WHO'S

HAUNTING

YOU?

WHO'S HAUNTING YOU?

by Shirley Bahlmann

© 2016 Shirley Bahlmann

ISBN: 978-0-9830503-9-1

Published by Grand Slam LLC

LIBRARY OF CONGRESS CATALOGING-IN-PUBLICATION DATA.
Who's Haunting You?: Firsthand accounts of interactions with the supernatural/complied by Shirley Bahlmann

p.cm

ISBN: 978-0-9830503-9-1
1. Supernatural 2. Occultism 3. Spirits I. Bahlmann, Shirley II. Title

Cover Design by Michael Hendarik Bahlmann
Cover Design © 2016 by Shirley Bahlmann
Cover Photo by Shirley Bahlmann

DEDICATION

For my son, Scott Dirk Bahlmann, who came up with terrific costumes for himself and his brothers, played some scary roles in theater, and is open to possibilities!

DISCLAIMER

This book was created from personal interviews. The stories are the sole responsibility of those who told them to me. I make no claims as to their truthfulness, I simply wrote them down.

ACKNOWLEDGEMENTS

Thanks to proofreaders Linda Floyd Pratt, Mary K. Olsen, Shelbie Young Ordakowski, and Scott Dirk Bahlmann for their help in finding frightful errors.

Also, thanks to Mike Ellerbeck of Salt Lake Monument for his endorsement of a prior book. He did not get the recognition he deserved, so here it is now:

Salt Lake Monument
186 North "N" Street
Salt Lake City, UT 84103
Phone 801-364-4025
Fax 801-364-4564
slmonument@gmail.com

TABLE OF CONTENTS:

Prologue: About Spirits
Melody Walker's insights to the Unseen

Melody Walker's been seeing auras since she was three years old. That's not surprising, since her mother could do the same thing. "They come in all different colors," Melody says. "A lot of times they change with mood. Surrounding colors in the world affect auras, too. For example, if a blue background is behind a green aura, the green and blue will blend together."

Of the three different aura levels, Melody usually sees the first one, which is just one color. If she concentrates, she can stretch it out to three different levels, which might include spiritual colors she's never seen before, because they don't exist in this life. When someone gets emotional, his or her aura grows brighter.

Melody once saw a lady whose aura was so dark that it looked like a black blob obscuring her face. Even though the lady was an actual person and not an evil spirit, Melody didn't want to get near her.

The ability to see auras is just one facet of Melody's rather uncommon abilities, because she's also able to see spirits. Experience has taught her what attracts the different types. High vibrations attract spirits of light, while low vibrations bring in malevolent entities.

Feeling depressed is a low vibration that attracts dark spirits. Attaching to the depression, the spirits hang around, making the person even more depressed. To keep this from happening, people should never berate themselves for anything they've done in the past. "Focus on the 'now' instead of 'then'," Melody says. "If you keep bringing up things you shouldn't have done, it's harder to forgive yourself. Instead, think of things you've repented of, and let yourself feel that you are worth it. When you think positively, you see yourself in a different way spiritually."

Melody sees a lot of church-going people struggle with unrealistic expectations, feeling they should get everything done. Then, if they don't finish their list, they may fall into depression. "We need to remember that we're human," Melody suggests.

Humans must be careful who their friends are, because people are inclined to attract friends on the same vibrational level. A person vibrating on a high level who spends a lot of time with a low level person tends to drop their vibration to match. Melody is quick to point out that it's fine to be friends with anyone, just keep in mind that spending a lot of time with others affects a person. Some people aren't the same on the inside as the outside. For example, a person who never misses a day of church may be on the same vibrational level as someone who's never stepped inside a church building.

Melody suggests keeping vibrational levels high, because humans can't get depressed in a state of high vibrational happiness. It may not be as difficult as some people may expect. One way to boost levels is to think positive thoughts about others, but be sure the thoughts aren't in the nature of, "It's nice that she's so pretty, but I'm so ugly." Comparing with others is not a good vibrational investment. Instead, realize that whatever abilities one has are not better or worse than others, they are just different.

Once vibrational levels are high, good things happen. Happy people who smile all the time raise vibrational levels. Even acting happy attracts good energy, and spirits of light and love move toward that happiness.

While it's easier and more enjoyable to hold onto light energy, many people are so used to being depressed and living in the dark that it's harder for them to look for and find the light. Dark energy comes around if people either invite it in or have made it a habit, but everyone has the power to raise their own vibrational levels.

One interesting feature that Melody is aware of are spiritual portals that can be opened wherever a person wants them. Light energy is free. The opposite is also true. Free dark energy allows low energy spirits to come through a portal, which can be opened with séances.

Spirit portals can even be on people. Melody admits to having one once. "It was on my back, which made it hurt," she said. Bad moods plagued her as she thought of extraordinarily vengeful witchcraft ways to get revenge on mean people. Even though she doesn't practice witchcraft, past family members have.

Melody was so disturbed by the images entering her mind that she told her mother, who said, "You're not actually thinking these things, because you don't have any personal knowledge of them." She invited Melody to pray with her, and they determined that every time Melody got mad, the portal on her opened, letting out a dark spirit that whispered things into her mind.

"I think people should be aware that these things can be put on you," Melody says. "The only way to get rid of them is to raise your vibrational levels to cast them out."

Melody has personally witnessed the spiritual

effects of the saying, "You stabbed me in the back." She's watched it happen when someone said or thought it. The result is physical or spiritual illness. With her spiritual sensitivity, Melody's experience of being "stabbed in the back" made her so sick that one of her kidneys shut down and she suffered migraines and nausea.

As another form of spiritual defense, people can raise shields of love and light to block evil energy. Each morning, Melody puts up pink shields for love and white-yellow ones for light. For a time she praying for shields, then realized she could raise them herself. She can also put them up around her family and anyone else who accepts them.

To install a shield at any time, simply use the power of words to state what is wanted. Held at a high vibration, no evil can get through a shield. Repetition and gratitude strengthen it, while negative thoughts dissolve it. A sign that something got through the shield is a person who feels depressed or anxious.

One of the strongest ways to get rid of things you don't want is with words. Words are purposeful, especially when combined with the name of a religious figure who is significant to the individual. "Say things like, 'I do not accept this, I am whole without it, it will go away,'" Melody suggests. "If you don't accept it, it can't be there." Prayer and fasting also raise vibrations.

Spirits are drawn to vibrations for different reasons. Some people who die suddenly are so distraught by the experience that they don't know they're dead, creating confusion in their spiritual state. This can be especially true for a young person who believes him or herself to be invincible.

After a rather stubborn sixteen-year-old boy died instantly in a car accident, Melody told his spirit that he was dead. He refused to accept it. It was only when he realized she was the only person acknowledging him that he began to consider that she might be right. He only believed it when he went to his own funeral.

Another man who died and came back to life described his experience as being metamorphosed into a blob of energy, which formed into a pink butterfly that flitted off to visit many worlds. Once the butterfly visited God the Father and Jesus Christ, it returned back to life in the form of the man.

"Everyone's death experience is as unique as each person's life," Melody explains.

Spirits can stay on the earth plane because they're attracted to things of this world, such as the case of a dead World War II veteran who was so attached to his uniform that his spirit stayed on earth, not wanting to leave it behind.

If an earth-bound spirit becomes willing to move on to the next life, he only needs to ask for someone to come and get him. "Christ is always there, waiting for anyone," Melody says.

A lot of times, people who've passed on before the deceased will hold a coming-out party for their loved one when they die, but no one is forced to go where they don't want to go, or be a certain way. Some people who may have been "terrific" a few years ago can change to the other side, and have no interest in returning to who they once were. At the final judgment, individuals decide where they end up. This system works nicely, because spirits don't want to be with those they aren't comfortable with any more than humans do.

The first dimension of death is for people who don't believe in life after death, so they wander the earth thinking they are still alive.

The next dimension is for those who had evil energies on earth and know they're dead, but want to stay where evil energy is. According to Melody, "A lot of people like being the bad person."

A third dimension belongs to spirits who move toward the light, which is often described as going through a tunnel to be with Christ or some other religious figure.

The earth also has different dimensions. Mortals are on the lowest rung, where good, evil, and mischievous spirits are mixed in with mankind. As the spiritual levels rise higher, certain entities are bumped out of the realm because they cannot ascend in the state they are in. Those on the lowest level can only see themselves, while mid-level dwellers can look down, but not up. The highest place hosts light and goodness, filled with high vibrational beings that can observe all the lower levels.

Since everything is connected on a spiritual plane, doing wrong not only brings your own spirit down, but can also affect your family line, not only for posterity, but also those who came before. That's what ancestral healing is for.

Melody's great great great grandfather was into witchcraft, actively casting spells and curses while in mortality. Even though he's dead, his spirit still lingers on earth. Since he still believes in witchcraft and doesn't want to change, the effects of his spiritual state still shadow the members of his family.

After receiving abuse at the hands of her father, his daughter, Mida, eventually married and had children, who had children, down to Melody's Aunt

Jill. Jill never experienced abuse, yet she's always been scared of men through the ancestral trauma inflicted on her great grandmother. This genetic code of abuse resulted in Jill never dating or marrying.

Melody had a milder case of ancestral fear of men until she went through a generational healing. During that experience, she discovered that Mida's spirit also wanted to be healed. Mida's decision to forgive her father also made it so that Melody is no longer afraid of men. Mida also fills a role as Melody's Guardian Angel.

Melody sees angels as an interesting safety feature for mortals. "Everyone has specific Guardian Angels for various situations," she says. Besides Mida, Melody identifies her angels as Sam, Zed, and Timothy. "Sam and Zed are here because I helped them before I came to earth," Melody explains. "Timothy came after I thought I'd found the man I would marry, who then told me he was homosexual. I was so upset that I decided to accept any man who would have me, no matter what he was like. To keep me from making a mistake, Timothy came, offering feelings of unconditional love and acceptance." Once Melody got past her neediness, Timothy left, since Guardian Angels can come and go as needed.

Sam and Zed appear when Melody feels like she needs more protection. At a time when she was conscious of making poor choices in her life, Zed came to her and said, "Melody, I can't make you stop, but I want you to know that what hurts you, hurts us." Caring more for her Guardian Angels than herself, Melody stopped what she was doing because she didn't want to hurt them.

By nature of their spiritual makeup, spirits have the ability to be in more than one place at a time.

With the power to protect many people simultaneously, angels use energy that is available all around us to provide protection on a spiritual level.

Melody's brother, Zane, was born on the same day of the year as his great grandfather, who is not only his Guardian Angel, but looks nearly identical to him. Zane is so spiritually gifted that he often feels claustrophobic when entering a room that appears empty to virtually everyone else, because there are so many spirits in there. While he's not afraid of spirits, he doesn't want to let people know he sees them, fearing that someone might put him in an insane asylum.

Everyone has different talents, gifts, and abilities. Everyone also has a choice in what they do with their life. Anyone can stay the same, or change. Thinking negatively about oneself is almost always a learned behavior, because babies are born loving themselves. It is through interpreting what other people say and do toward a person that can change that person's perception of himself or herself. People are able to learn to control their thoughts and actions, which can move them toward something worse, or something better. There are spirits willing to help mortals head in either direction. All one needs to do is ask.

Spirits in the House and Out

Melody Walker saw her first ghost as a toddler living in Arizona. Initially, she just felt a dark sensation every time she left her bedroom to walk down the stairs to the main floor. Things got spookier the night she woke up to see a man standing beside her bed. To a three-year-old, he was frighteningly big, six feet tall, with dark brown hair. Terrified, Melody wondered what he was going to do to her. When he simply stared at her, the tension finally drained the little girl's emotional reserves and she escaped back into sleep.

When Melody woke up again, it was still night, and the man was still standing there. Since falling asleep hadn't gotten rid of him, this time little Melody mustered the courage to get out of bed on the opposite side from the figure. As soon as her feet hit the floor, she rushed downstairs, crying, "Mommy! There's a man in my room!"

Her mother went upstairs to check, but the man was gone. Melody climbed back in bed and fell asleep, but just before dawn, she opened her eyes to see the man watching her again.

The nightly visits went on for a week before the man finally stopped appearing.

When Melody was eight, her mother asked her one day, "Do you remember that man that used to stand by your bed at night?"

"Yeah."

"He stood by my bed, too," her mother admitted. "I finally cast him out of the house."

That explained why he left, but Melody couldn't help wondering what had brought the man to her bedside in the first place. She never found out.

Her next experience was a happier one when she became aware of a spirit woman in the extra bedroom beside hers. The spirit wore a sweeping white dress and a crown of fresh flowers and leaves on top of her long black hair. When she sang, Melody sang along with her. Unlike the man in the night, this spirit made Melody feel content.

When her brother moved into the extra bedroom, things changed in a hurry. Her brother claimed that he couldn't go in his room because of her. "She only sings," Melody said in defense of her next door neighbor.

"She did until I started cleaning my gun in there," her brother said. "Then she got really upset."

In an effort to help, Melody approached the ghost, now manifesting wilted flower petals sliding down her unkempt hair as she rocked back and forth with her head in her hands.

"What's wrong?" Melody asked.

"Your brother has a gun," the ghost said in a mournful whisper.

"We have lots of guns," Melody answered.

"It's not okay to have a gun here," the ghost insisted, yet she refused to tell Melody why. She remained a sad spirit before gradually fading away.

When Melody was fifteen, her family established a favorite walking route up a long hill and down a left hand turn toward a river running alongside the path. They enjoyed the novelty of feeding apples to a few curious horses in a pasture along the route. Even though it was an idyllic stretch of road, Melody always had a feeling that there was something wrong on the part of the trail that paralleled the river.

One day when she returned from a walk, her

mother turned to stare at her. Then Mom said, "I think someone followed you home."

Curious, Melody went to her room, sat down and "tuned in," which means that she listened closely until she tuned in to a middle aged man wearing khaki colored pants and a shirt that looked like a blouse. By asking questions, she learned that he'd been alive in the early 1900's, and was still looking for his daughter who'd gone out for a walk and never returned home.

"It turned out that she had drowned in the same river we passed on our walks," Melody says. "The man's spirit recognized me because my grandpa was the one who found the girl's body."

Once she told the spirit the reason he was still in the mortal plane, a problem arose. He refused to believe he was dead. "It's hard to explain to someone that they are dead," Melody says. "He had to accept it in order to move on."

But the father was not about to accept it, and was so angry that Melody had even suggested such a preposterous idea that he promptly disappeared.

A week later, he was back, admitting that Melody was probably right. At that point, Melody's suggestions helped him cross over.

Melody discovered that the father's spirit had stayed behind to find his daughter, but who was the man standing by Melody in the night? Was he a former home owner who couldn't understand why there were strangers in the beds?

Was he somehow connected to the woman with flowers in her hair? Had he been the one whose gun had frightened her so badly?

Rachel Green's Ghosts

Blonde, blue-eyed Rachel Green was ten years old when her family moved into a cute two-story house painted white as milk. While exploring their new home, Rachel decided to play Hide and Seek with her twelve year old half brother, dark-skinned, black-haired Malachi. Their other brother and three sisters joined in the game, too, and Malachi volunteered to be "It."

Looking for a place to hide, Rachel hurried upstairs and was delighted to find a little closet door. She opened it, ready to squeeze in before shutting it behind her, when she noticed a little girl staring out at her with a pair of bright blue eyes. The family Hide and Seek rule was that two people couldn't hide in the same place at once. Disappointed that her eight-year-old sister, Sara, had already claimed the hiding place, Rachel shut the door.

Just as she turned away to search for another hiding spot, Rachel stopped with a sudden frightening realization. The eyes she'd seen were too blue to be Sara's.

Rachel whipped around and yanked the door open. The eyes were gone, along with the girl.

Rachel pounded down the stairs, calling, "Malachi! Malachi!"

"Found you!" Malachi cried with a grin, reaching out and tagging Rachel's shoulder.

"There's a ghost in the house," Rachel gasped.

Her brother's eyes widened for just a second before he burst into laughter. "Sure, Rachel. But you're still 'It.'"

"She was upstairs in the little closet," Rachel

insisted.

Malachi's eyes shifted toward the stairs, then back to Rachel. Putting on a condescending smile, he asked, "Which closet? There's got to be more than one up there."

"The little one right in the hallway. Go look for yourself." Rachel shuddered. "She disappeared once, but maybe she's back again."

For a moment, it looked as if Malachi would make up some excuse not to go investigate, but suddenly he turned and leaped up the stairs, two at a time. Rachel stared up after him, unwilling to go with him and risk looking into those haunting blue eyes again.

Malachi returned a couple of minutes later, charging down the stairs two at a time, looking as pale as his dark skin allowed. He'd lost lost his mocking smile.

"What did you see?" Rachel asked.

"I told you, there's no such thing as ghosts."

"Really?" Rachel asked. "I think you saw something up there."

"No ghosts." Malachi turned and left the room and the game.

Rachel suspected he was lying, especially after her sisters reported that a little girl with blonde hair and intense blue eyes joined them while they were watching TV. Each one assumed she was a new friend of a different sister, so none of them thought it strange until she disappeared.

One evening, Rachel turned away from washing dishes at the kitchen sink to see a blonde girl with blue eyes watching her from the doorway. At first glance, she thought it was one of her sisters. When she realized the girl had the same intense blue eyes

Rachel had seen in the closet, she wasn't afraid, just uncertain about what to do. When the girl noticed Rachel watching her, she faded away.

When the family moved away from that house, Rachel was relieved to think they'd left the little ghost girl behind. She was wrong. Rachel was stunned to see the Sara-look-alike again at the next house, then the next.

"We've been seeing the same girl over and over no matter where we move," Rachel says. "She honestly looks like my sister, but she doesn't age."

In trying to figure out why the ghost girl followed them, Rachel recalled that her mother had a miscarriage when Rachel was nearly two years old, before Sara was born.

Was the little girl the miscarried baby? If so, having found her family at last, did she decide to take part in her family's activities?

The blue-eyed ghost was not Rachel's only encounter with the supernatural. When Rachel was a teenager, a visit to her new friend, Denae's house, had her darting glances over her shoulder where she thought she could see shadows slipping along the walls, as indistinct as fish sliding through murky water. Yet when Rachel stared at the movement, everything stilled. Rachel had the uneasy sense that curious eyes stared at the back of her head.

This unsettling event happened the next couple of times she stopped at Denae's, too. It wasn't a very happy house. After Denae's brother drowned in a heartbreaking accident, her parents divorced and Denae lived with her mother. The whole situation was hard on 15-year-old Denae, and was only made worse by the fact that her mother dated a guy who kept forgetting to shave or put on deodorant.

On the last day Rachel ever crossed Denae's threshold, she wondered if her visits to help cheer Denae up were really helping, or if Denae would be better off seeing someone like a counselor.

While Denae went to get a couple of sodas, Rachel caught a movement from the edge of her vision that looked like trickling wetness creeping across the edges of the ceiling. When she looked, again there was nothing to see, but Denae's voice sounded from the doorway. "What're you looking at?"

Rachel swiped her hand through the air as if brushing away cobwebs. "Nothing."

"If it's nothing, then why are you looking?"

Suddenly cold, Rachel rubbed her arms. "I thought I saw something, but it must have been headlight reflections."

"It's the middle of the afternoon." Denae's knowing smile as she handed Rachel a soda gave Rachel the creeps. "Headlights wouldn't show up on the ceiling unless it was dark."

Wishing she'd stayed home, Rachel popped the lid on her soda can and took a drink, letting the cold bubbles flow down her throat so fast that her eyes watered. She pulled the can away and swiped at her eyes. "Maybe I'm just tired."

Denae leaned closer and said in an intense whisper, "Or maybe you're finally seeing them."

"Seeing who?" Rachel looked over her shoulder. "I thought we the only ones here."

Denae hunched her shoulders as if trying to keep someone from overhearing. "We're the only ones here except the ghosts."

A ripple of alarm slipped up Rachel's spine. "I didn't see any ghosts."

"Are you sure? What were you looking at?"

Suddenly exasperated, Rachel set her can down with one hand and flung out her other arm. "Nothing!"

Denae's chin lowered until she was staring at Rachel from beneath her bangs. "You know you saw something. It's the ghosts."

Deciding to humor her friend, Rachel forced herself to speak calmly. "What ghosts, Denae?"

"The ones that follow me."

"Why would they follow you?"

Denae's mouth curved into an eerie smile that made her look like a stranger. "They protect me."

"From what?"

"Danger. Water, mostly."

Rachel rubbed her head, wishing she'd changed the subject.

"They all hate water, all eight of them," Denae murmured.

Rachel's head came up. "Eight?"

Denae watched Rachel intently for a moment before slowly nodding. "They all drowned, you see." A shadow slid along the wall behind Denae, followed quickly by another that went in the opposite direction, flowing as smoothly as seaweed caught in a current. "I'm glad you can finally see them, too."

"I don't!" Rachel jumped to her feet. "Oh, my goodness, look at the time. I've got to go now."

Denae watched her silently for five long beats, then said, "Next time I'll introduce you to them properly."

"We'll see," Rachel answered as she headed for the door, intending to never come back.

As Rachel slipped through the door, a sudden thought sent ice through her veins. What if those weird shadows followed Denae wherever she went? Were they really ghosts? Or was Denae's story just a way for her to cope with the unfortunate circumstances in her life? pretty good but unsatisfied

Through subsequent experiences, Rachel determined that the time between midnight and 3:00 am is the "Witching Hour," when paranormal activity as well as crime rates go up.

When Rachel was eighteen, she went to bed after midnight, when her sister was already sleeping peacefully in the other bed across the room. Rachel woke up during the Witching Hour from the sound of footsteps crossing her bedroom floor. Her first thought, *Okay, that's weird,* was followed by a paralyzing sense of fear. A self-proclaimed "Scaredy Cat," Rachel only moved her eyes to gaze around the dark room with the hope that the sound was her sister walking across the floor on her nightly foray into the bathroom, but the unfamiliar footfalls didn't head that direction. Instead, they trod closer to Rachel's bed.

Heart hammering, Rachel shut her eyes just before the bed dipped from something sitting on the mattress next to her hip. The sound of its breathing filled her with fear, which mounted as pressure that felt like a hand pushed down on her chest. After a thumb-like appendage pressed on her throat, the only sound of breathing came from the thing, because Rachel couldn't draw in any air. The thing leaned closer and whispered, "You have to listen to me, listen to me."

It shifted on the bed, pressing down on her lungs, repeating its spooky phrase. "You have to listen to me, listen to me."

Desperate for air, Rachel tried to call her sister for help, but as soon as she opened her mouth, the pressure on her throat increased. Frantic, Rachel tried with all her might to get her sister's attention, silently struggling in the wild hope that her sister would wake up and save her.

Suddenly, the mattress lifted, putting her bed back to normal, and she drew in a noisy lungful of air. The thing on her bed was gone.

Too terrified to open her eyes in case something was staring down at her from beside her bed, she lay as still as if she were dead until morning.

Rachel is convinced that the thing wasn't her little sister playing a trick on her. For one thing, her sister wasn't strong enough to hold her down. For another thing, why would she do it?

What did the thing want Rachel to listen to? Rachel doesn't know, because she didn't hear it say anything besides, "Listen to me, listen to me." Could it have been a spirit passing by in the Witching Hour, looking for someone who wasn't deeply asleep to tell something to? Was Rachel struggling too much for the thing to deliver its message? Was it the spirit of someone who'd died of asphyxiation? Rachel may never know. She's just glad it left before she suffocated.

Ninety Years In a Haunted House

Enid was seven years old when her parents moved their family of girls into a house on Main Street in 1927. The sturdy, two-story brick had a lovely wrap around porch, but inside, Enid and her sisters were put to work tidying unkempt rooms and scrubbing dirty floors. The family that just moved out was made up of girls, too, except for the youngest - a boy whose mother died when he was born.

Enid didn't known the previous owner's children very well, and had never met the father. From all reports, he was not a nice man. Not only was he stingy with his money, he refused to allow his children to act like children. He forbade them entrance to the front rooms of the house, shutting them behind the sliding glass pocket doors, relegating them to the kitchen, mud room, and upstairs bedrooms. The oldest daughter did her best to care for the younger children, but she was still a child herself. When she was eighteen, their father died.

The neighbor lady reported that on the night of his death, his children turned on every light in the house and danced through the rooms upstairs, downstairs, even sliding open the pocket doors to cavort through the forbidden front rooms. It was a real celebration.

Enid didn't know what happened when the children moved out, but she likes to think the money from selling the house helped them move on with their lives, and that they continued to take care of each other.

It appears that their father may not have been inclined to move on.

When Enid's grandson, Joseph, lived with her

while attending the local Snow College, he found himself trying to make a decision about whether to get married to a cute co-ed he'd fallen in love with, or whether to spend two years abroad in religious service. Lying on his bed to mulli the situation over didn't bring him answers. Instead, he suddenly felt as if someone grabbed him by the throat and squeezed. Gasping for air, he was conscious enough to note that he was alone in the room, at least as far as he could see. Only when he commanded whatever entity held him to leave him alone in the name of Jesus Christ did the pressure ease up on his neck and he was able to breathe freely.

Was it possible that the widower was taking his frustration out on Joseph? Was he angry at his children's misbehavior, or because Joseph was close to marriage and the widower's wife had been taken, leaving him with all the children?

Enid grew up, married Wayne Graser, purchased her childhood home, and raised their children there. When Wayne retired, Enid discovered a new passion for ocean cruises. She loved every minute, from the endless buffets to the entertainment to standing on deck and breathing in the brisk ocean air to the maid doing all the cleaning and leaving a delectable chocolate on her pillow. Enid would have stayed longer if she could, but at the end of seven glorious days, she had to depart.

Walking reluctantly walk down the exit ramp, Enid was startled by a shout of, "Smile!" just before a flash made her blink. A grinning photographer appeared from behind a camera and offered to make her souvenir Alaskan cruise photo into a keepsake. What would Enid like? A mug? A t-shirt? A magnet? A keychain?

Wayne was indifferent, so Enid chose the keychain and carried her happy memory home with her. After fastening her car key on the Alaskan cruise keychain for frequent reminders of her unforgettable trip, she tossed it into the basket by the back door where all their keys were kept. Every time Enid got in her car to run an errand, the keychain stirred fond memories of her charmed life at sea.

A short time later, her husband passed away.

Enid's children rallied around her, taking her where she needed to go until after the services. Once they went home, Enid sifted through the keys in the basket so she could drive to the store, but she didn't see the Alaskan Cruise keychain. She looked through again, but it was still missing. She always put her keys in the basket, so where was it?

Then she noticed what looked like her car key fastened on a free promotional keychain from the local hardware store. She'd never noticed that particular keychain before. She rarely went to that store, but her husband was a frequent visitor. When she picked it up, she saw a key that looked like it belonged to her car. She tested it, and her car started on the first try.

Who had taken her Alaskan Cruise souvenir and put her key on a different keychain? With her husband gone, she was the only one in the house, and she locked her doors. She walked around the house, checking for other signs of theft, but found nothing else missing.

Then she thought that perhaps one of her children had taken it for a souvenir. When she called and asked them, they were each as puzzled as she was. Had an extended family member taken it? It didn't seem likely, but she asked them, too. No one confessed. They'd never lied to her before, so she was inclined to believe them.

Enid searched high and low, going through every place in her house systematically, but she never found the missing souvenir. She couldn't help but wonder if her husband may have somehow spirited it away, since he often played tricks on her. If it was him, she's glad that he at least left her the car key.

Another mysterious incident occurred when Enid stood in the doorway of her upstairs guest room, staring in dismay at the papers strewn across the floor. She'd cleaned this room just two days earlier when her granddaughter left, so where had all these papers come from?

Stepping inside the room, Enid picked up a loose page and discovered that they belonged in her daughter's old loose leaf journal. The binder lay open nearby, its three rings gaping open in an eerie silver smile.

How could this have happened? Enid shivered at the thought of someone breaking into her house and creeping upstairs to this room. That didn't seem likely, though. She always locked her doors, even in the daytime. Besides, why would a burglar bother to scatter papers around and leave everything else alone? As Enid gathered up the pages, she wondered if the binder had somehow fallen from the bookshelf, the impact springing the rings open. That might make the pages loose, but why would they scatter? She checked the window. Closed. Then her eyes caught sight of a body-sized dent on top off the mussed bedspread. Enid's memory of smoothing the bedspread two days earlier was clear. But no one had been in her home since she'd cleaned this room.

After making a mess of the guest room, whatever

it was seemed to move downstairs to do its mischief in the living room. A portrait of Enid's grandfather-in-law, decorated with the old gentleman's horsehair keychain watch fob, had hung in its place on the wall for years. One night after Enid had just settled into bed, she heard the sound of a solid *clunk.*

Wondering at the strange sound, Enid got up and flicked on the light. When she walked into the living room, she found great-grandpa's picture on the floor. Puzzled, she moved closer and saw that the nail was still in the wall. When she touched it, it was solidly fixed in the plaster. She couldn't even wiggle it.

That was strange. How had the photo fallen from its sturdy nail?

After re-hanging the picture, Enid gave it a tug to test that it was firmly hung up before she went back to bed.

Her efforts weren't enough. Although it stayed in place throughout the day, on subsequent nights, the falling picture woke her more than once. The nail was always firmly set, yet the picture was on the floor. Finally Enid asked her children for help. Once the photo was firmly fixed to the wall with screws, it stopped falling down in the night.

One night Enid's visiting children sat around the living room talking of old times when Enid noticed a white gossamer shape floating through the room. Wide-eyed, she tore her gaze from the vaguely human shape and glanced at her daughter, Michelle. Michelle was staring back at her. Then Michelle's eyes darted to the suspended figure and back to her mother. No one else seemed to notice the apparition.

Later, Enid and Michelle talked about the floating figure, verifying that each of them had seen the same thing. Enid felt a sense of peace, as if a departed family member had come back to listen to them talk of old times.

Is it possible that since her husband was missing out on life, he didn't want to miss out on the happy memories that went with it, so he took the keychain?

Could there have been a ghost in the guest room? If so, who was it? What did it want?

Was it Great Grandpa? Had he read his great-great granddaughter's journal with such interest that he didn't watch where he flung the pages? Had he tried to move his own photo? When he couldn't move the picture, did he decide to make a personal appearance?

Long White Hair

Randy Christiansen grew up in a house with a staircase that led not only to his bedroom, but also to a really long hallway that was a great place for pretending. Six-year-old Randy imagined the hall was a walkway to a space ship hatch, or the street of a wild west town where he faced off with another gunfighter at the other end, or the entry to a circus ring. It didn't occur to Randy to imagine the hallway as a ghost portal until the day he saw the old lady with long white hair.

That was the day Randy went upstairs to go to his room, but stopped on the landing when he saw a stranger at the end of the hall. Her long white hair flowed down over the back of her white dress, the hem brushing the floor as she crossed the hall at the far end and disappeared from view. It looked as if she'd walked from one bedroom to another, but the doors were closed, and she hadn't stopped to turn a doorknob. How could she have gone through a closed door without opening it?

As Randy puzzled over what he'd seen, he thought that the woman looked a little bit like his great grandmother, who lived in a different city. Randy went in search of his mother. "Mom, is Great Grandma visiting?"

"Visiting who?"

"Is she upstairs visiting us?"

"No, she's not here," his mother said. "Why are you asking?"

"I saw a lady upstairs, and it looked like her."

"A lady? Where?"

Randy showed her where he'd seen the woman with long white hair, but no one was there. Since his story was treated with a large dose of skepticism, Randy stopped stopped talking about it, but that wasn't the last time Randy crossed the path of the lady with the long white hair.

Six years later, Great Grandma had passed away and Randy's family was living in a different house. He and his sister fell asleep one night on their father's chaise lounge. Randy woke up early in the morning with a sense that someone else was there. Sitting up, he saw the same old woman in white kneeling at the end of the chaise, hands in prayer pose, close enough for him to see her wrinkles when she lifted her head. Her long white hair shifted on her shoulders as she looked him right in the eye.

Weak with fear, Randy fell back down not the chaise and tried to shake his sister awake. A fearful glance at the end of the chaise assured him that the woman was gone. There hadn't been time for her to walk out of the room. She had simply vanished.

Randy didn't tell his family about his second sighting. They hadn't believed him before, so why would they listen to him now?

Did Great Grandma have a mysterious twin sister? Or was it someone else in the family tree checking up on her descendants, or taking it upon herself to remind them to say their prayers before going to sleep?

Oh, That Ghost

When eleven-year-old Taylor Soper was home in the basement watching TV, the computer on the other end of the room suddenly turned itself on, *bsssrrr*. Startled, Taylor jumped up, but didn't see anyone else in the room with him. *What the heck?* He ran upstairs to see if someone had come home when he wasn't looking.

There was no one else there.

Creeping back down the stairs, Taylor kept his eye on the computer, which was now inexplicably turned off. How could that be if no one was there to push the "off" button? For that matter, how in the world had it turned on by itself in the first place?

When his family came home, Taylor told them what happened, but no one had a reasonable explanation.

Intrigued, his big brother, Austin, tried to recreate the computer turning on and off without using hands, but nothing he and Taylor tried worked.

After that day, Austin had several experiences

where the computer screen lit up as though someone had jiggled the mouse when no one was near the computer table.

Taylor's next electronic mishap was even more bizarre. His parents gave him his own mobile phone with the condition that he not take it to school. So he put his phone on his bedside stand when he left for school with his brothers and sisters. At the same time, his parents went to work.

When Taylor returned home for lunch, he checked his phone for messages. There were none, but to his amazement, he found a video recording of his ceiling, accompanied by a strange, ghostly hum. The phone had not been moved from its spot. It had simply been turned on in the middle of the morning, recorded the ceiling for twenty minutes, and then turned off.

Taylor asked everyone in the household which one of them had come home early and messed with his phone. No one had. When they watched the video evidence and listened to the faint, steady noise, no one could tell if it was a ghostly voice or an electronic hum.

Excited for a new mystery, the brothers tried setting ghost traps, such as leaving various other objects in Taylor's room, but nothing else was tampered with.

Strange things also happened in other parts of the house. The boys' mother, Karen, was home alone one day getting ready for work. As she put on makeup in the bathroom adjacent to the back bedroom, she was startled by three distinct knocks on the shared wall.

Wondering who was home, Karen walked into the hall and checked the bedroom. No one was there, so she walked through the house and found it empty.

That's weird.

With no more time to investigate, she hurried back into the bathroom to finish getting ready.

Knock, knock, knock.

This time, Karen walked out of the bathroom and called, "Ghost, I know you're here, now let me get ready."

The knocking stopped.

Another time when Karen was reading the newspaper in the kitchen, the cupboard door in the laundry room slammed shut, making her jump. *What the heck?* Karen went to check the laundry room, which is next to the back bedroom, but no cupboards were open. She returned to her newspaper. *Slam!*

Oh, that ghost.

"Okay," Karen said aloud, "I acknowledge your presence."

After that, the cupboard door stopped opening and slamming shut of its own accord.

Karen's husband, Korry, had his own experience with the mysterious presence. When he was in the kitchen by himself, he caught sight of a figure hurrying down the hall toward the back bedroom, accompanied by the sound of quick, running footfalls. Wondering if Taylor had unexpectedly come home, Korry went to check.

The back bedroom was empty. Korry investigated the whole house, looking for another living being, but he was the only one home.

One night, the whole family, including daughters Whitney and Ashley, witnessed an unexplained event while sitting at the table eating Sunday dinner. Their conversation was interrupted by the sudden slam of the back bedroom door.

Austin and Taylor led the way to the door and opened it onto an empty room. The closed windows meant that no cross breeze could have blown the door shut. Besides, that particular door tended to catch on the carpet instead of swinging freely, so it needed to be pulled closed.

When the rest of the family left the scene, Austin and Taylor couldn't help wondering how the door had slammed shut on its own. They conducted experiments, leaving it open and trying to make it close without touching it.

They couldn't do it. There was no logical explanation for the door to shut of its own accord. After that, the brothers decided to leave the door open all the time, inviting whatever force had slammed it closed to do it again.

Whatever is causing the mysterious happenings, it seems to want interaction with the Soper's, or at least to be acknowledged. In a quest for more information, Korry, Taylor, and Austin started watching the "Ghost Adventures" show.

When Austin married, he and he and his wife, Laney, lived with Korry and Karen for a summer. Not long after moving in, Laney asked if something weird was going on in the house. Then she got to hear all of the ghost stories.

Austin and Laney's daughter is a little leery of Grandma and Grandpa's house, too, but the one she lives in has an unexplained incident that happened after Austin and Laney put their two children to bed. The parents went downstairs, but it wasn't long before they heard footfalls running around in the upstairs toy room.

Thinking their children had gotten out of bed and snuck out of their room to play. Austin went upstairs to put them back. To his surprise, they weren't in the toy room. Mystified, Austin checked their bedroom, where they both lay sound asleep.

Austin called the landlord to see if anyone else who'd lived in the house had experienced paranormal experiences. The landlord told Austin he didn't know of any, but generations of his family had lived in the house for over a hundred years, so there could be something there.

Wondering about his experiences with paranormal events in two different houses, Austin says, "I don't know if it's me or what."

Because of all the unexplained events he grew up with, Austin sees his whole family as being open to the possibility of supernatural occurrences. A willingness to consider their existence makes it more likely that his family recognizes them. Austin is never afraid of unexplained happenings, and no one in his family seems to be afraid of peculiar occurrences, either.

"When something weird happens, we always refer to our ghost," Karen says. "It's just like we have someone else in the house that should be paying rent."

If there is a ghost, who is it? One theory is that it could be an elderly guest who died in the back bedroom when the house belonged to the former owner, Marilyn Anderson, who occasionally operated a bed and breakfast business in her home.

A more popular candidate is the Soper's elderly neighbor, Albert Antrei. Before he passed away in 2001, he would talk to the Soper's over the fence. Occasionally, he complained of Marilyn as being an "indifferent" lady. Albert and his wife, Iona, had sold Marilyn the property next door to them in Manti, Utah. The Antrei's understanding was that she'd build her house far enough back on the lot so the mountain views were unobstructed from Antrei's windows. Instead, Marilyn built it right in the middle of their view. Interestingly enough, there is a completely clear view of the mountains from the Soper's back bedroom, where most of the oddities have taken place.

Albert was an educated man, a former high school principal who was born in Belgium. A linguist and a writer, he was curious about the world and how things work. It makes perfect sense that he would want to fiddle with modern day electronics to see what they can do.

Another reason that Albert is the favored possibility is that Austin doesn't remember anything unexplained happening in the house until Albert passed away a few years after his wife died.

One of the most frustrating incidents happened in 2015 when Karen drove home, parked her car in the garage, and closed the garage door. She left her brand new iPhone on the front passenger seat so she could meet with a group of young women in her house without distracting phone calls.

When the group left, Karen went to the car to retrieve her phone, but it was gone.

Looking in the door pockets, under all the seats, and even the glove box did not bring the phone to light. Korry tried to help by calling Karen's number, but her phone didn't ring. How could that be? It was fully charged and turned on. Korry conducted his own search, doing everything but pulling the panels off the doors, but he couldn't find it, either. When Karen tried tracking her phone through the Apple company, the listing came up as completely offline. "Apple can't believe it," Karen says. "They said, 'This is so strange. Even if it's off, we can usually track it.'"

There seems to be no reasonable explanation for the phone to go missing from the Soper's closed garage and suddenly become untrackable. If it was spirited away, maybe the company's tracking system doesn't reach as far as the phone's new owner.

One incident seems to indicate that either the ghost is a woman, or there is more than one wandering around the Soper's house. In June of 2015, Ashley and her husband, Connor Dyreng, were staying with Karen and Korry. Whitney asked Ashley to watch her three-year-old, Maddax, while Whitney went to girls' camp for a few days. Ashley agreed.

Karen was at work as school principal when Ashley and Connor put Maddax to bed in Whitney's old room. This was no small task, because ever since he was one year old, Maddax has been terrified of that basement bedroom. To make matters worse, he missed his parents, which gave him energy to fight against going to sleep.

At last, Ashley and Connor lay down on either side of Maddax to keep him contained and offer comfort. Just as his cries reduced to soft sighs, and his little body relaxed enough that his eyes closed, a woman's voice called out in a prolonged sing-song voice, "Maaa-daaax!"

Maddax's eyes flew open wide and he sat up, crying, "Mommy!"

"No, honey, that wasn't your mommy," Ashley said. Why on earth had her mother called his name as soon as she got home? Maybe she wondered where he was, but she didn't need to shout.

As Maddax cried harder and tried to get off the bed to look for Mommy, Ashley said to Connor, "You stay here and get him settled down again. I'm going to talk to Mom."

Ashley marched upstairs. She couldn't find Karen anywhere, but she saw her father reading in his room. "Where's Mom?"

"At work."

Puzzled, Ashley said, "We heard someone call Maddax. What it you?"

"No. Why would I?"

"I thought it was Mom, but she couldn't have if she's not home."

"It wasn't me, either."

Ashley went back downstairs. "Connor, you heard someone calling Maddax, didn't you?"

"Yes. What did your mom say?"

"She's not here." Neither of them could figure out where the voice came from.

The next day, Ashley called Whitney to tell her of the strange event. Whitney was astonished. "That's crazy," she said. "Is Maddax all right?"

Ashley assured her that he was, but neither sister could come up with an explanation for the phenomenon.

Whitney had her own unexplained event when she and her husband, Kurt Marchant, visited her childhood home with Maddax just before Halloween in 2015. They all slept in Whitney's old bedroom, but Whitney woke up in the night to the sound of Maddax whimpering. When she saw her little boy wandering around the room, she sat up and asked, "Maddax, what's wrong, honey?"

Turning his tear-filled eyes towed her, he said forlornly, "The ghost, the ghost."

With a sudden chill, Whitney asked, "Where is the ghost?"

Maddax pointed toward the ceiling. "Up there, flying high."

When Ashley heard the story, she was so upset that she told her father the house needed to be blessed. She also couldn't help wondering if the ghost was the culprit in the case of her missing wedding ring.

In December of 2013, Ashley and Connor stayed at the house while everyone else was out of town. After eating dinner, Ashley took off her wedding ring to wash the dishes. When she was done, the couple went in the other room to watch TV.

Before bed, Ashley returned to the kitchen to get her ring, but it was gone. "I thought I'd put it on the windowsill or counter," Ashley said, "but it was nowhere to be seen." First they searched all the obvious places, and then turned the house upside down, including pulling up rugs and taking drains apart. They didn't find the ring. Next, they called the police and checked pawn shops, but the ring never turned up. "It was completely gone," Ashley said.

When the Soper brothers had another run-in with the ghost, they were fortunate not to lose any of their elk hunting gear. Austin and Taylor were in the basement of their parents' home on November 20, 2015, packing for an elk hunt while their mother was out running errands with Austin's children. The brothers were nearly done when they heard footsteps overhead, along with an indistinct voice. "Mom's back," Austin announced.

"Oh, great," Taylor moaned. "Now your son's going to be upset, because he's too little to go with us."

"No, he'll be fine," Austin assured Taylor as he gathered up his hunting gear. "He wants to stay at Grandma's house." Taylor picked up his things and they trooped upstairs to say goodbye.

No one was there. Karen's car was not parked outside or in the garage.

Puzzled, Austin turned to Taylor. "Did you hear footsteps?"

"Yeah," Taylor answered, "and a voice."

"What did it say?"

"I couldn't make out the words," Taylor said, dropping his things on the floor and heading for the room where a mysterious recording had been left on his phone years earlier, and the door had slammed shut with no explanation. "We were right under this room." Taylor opened the door to an empty room.

"I could have sworn I heard someone walking," Austin said.

"Me, too."

They looked at each other, and then said with sardonic grins, "Oh, that ghost."

Could all of the electrical problems be odd glitches in the house's wiring? Or is Albert figuring out how the newfangled things work? One reason given for ghosts staying around is strong emotions. Could Albert still be so annoyed at Marilyn for building her house in a place that blocked his mountain view that he comes back to look out the window that lets him see the vista he once enjoyed from his house?

What about the slamming doors? Does Albert still like his neighbors' company so much he wants to keep interacting with them? Or is it as Karen says, "I wonder if Albert's watching over this house."

Who is the fearful ghost Maddax saw flying up high? Was it the same one that called to him in a woman's voice? If there's a female spirit in the house, did she take Ashley's wedding ring?

What created the sound of footsteps and a voice in the upstairs bedroom while the brothers got ready for their hunt? Was it something wanting to join them? Or something waiting for them to leave?

The Dark Man
Andrew Bahlmann

The day my wife, Heidi, and I pulled in front of our new apartment building in Cedar City, Utah was memorable in its own right. We left the familiar behind and drove down with all our possessions packed in a large horse trailer. Though it wasn't ominous, the building was less than we were hoping for. Something seemed a little off. But, sight unseen, we had signed a contract and things didn't seem all that bad. So we unloaded with the help of our family, settled our young son into his nursery, and got ready to start at a new school all on our own.

Southern Utah University was a change from Snow College in Ephraim, Utah, where we met and were married. Now we were farther away from family than we had ever been and couldn't rely on them like we had in the past. But we dove in, made the most of it, and began to enjoy our new life on our own.

We found out a little more about what it meant to be on our own one dark night.

We tended to sleep with the doors to our bedroom and the nursery open so we could navigate to our son's crib without having to deal with doors while only semi-awake. The night in question, I was lying in bed, beginning to drift off, but with my eyes still pointed in the general direction of our bedroom door.

What I saw in the hallway was so unexpected that it caused a physical reaction, sending chills rippling through my body.

Whatever was moving through the hall had the general shape of a man, with the recognizable outline of head and shoulders, as if it were shrouded in a heavy black cloak. It appeared as a thick shadow towering at least eight feet tall. I could see no real features, no face, arms, or legs, but it appeared to be a dark man.

The figure seemed to pause for a moment in the hall outside our door, then slipped into the nursery.

I was ready to pass it off as nothing more than a shadow made into something more by a half-awake mind when my wife whispered, "Did you see that?" The strain in her voice made it clear that she was talking about the same thing I had seen.

We quickly moved from our bed to the side of our child's crib. As I stepped through the doorway, I didn't know what to expect and wasn't sure how I would react, but it turned out there was nothing in the room besides our son.

Heidi scooped him up and held him close while I checked the windows in the room. They were shut and locked. The closet was empty and there was nowhere else in the room that thing could have gone.

We decided to kneel and pray in that room, inviting the spirit of God to dispel the fear and darkness we felt after seeing the substantial shadow in our home. That night, our son slept in our bed.

Though we never had an experience like that again, we learned that one of the apartments was host to a drug den. Occasionally, we heard scuffling in the hall, but nothing ever crossed our threshold. One morning after a nighttime police visit, we found smears and spatters of blood on the walls of the stairwell that led to our apartment.

As soon as our lease was over we found a new place to live and had no regrets leaving that place behind.

Though we don't think about it much, sometimes I wonder - was the figure just a shadow seen though sleepy eyes? Was the shadow linked to what was going on in other apartments, or had something happened in our own place that invited the shadow in? Was it drawn to my son, or a specific room that needed a spiritual fumigation?

Where Are Your Children?

Before 2014, thirty-two year old Bob Aguado would have told anyone that it was impossible for ghosts to appear. Once people were dead, they were dead.

Some of his coworkers at the turkey plant in Moroni, Utah, insisted that the spirits of their three departed coworkers were still in the plant, but Bob didn't believe them. Instead, he aggravated some of the people he worked with by walking the halls, calling out in a sing-song voice, "Oh, Juan, where are you? Mike, come out, come out, wherever you are! Hey, Bruce, if you're really here, then show yourself!"

One man shook his head at Bob with foreboding, along with the promise, "You'll be sorry."

A young woman pointed at Bob with the warning, "Be careful what you say, or one of these days, someone's going to get you."

"No way," Bob scoffed. "Spirits don't come back after the person dies."

"You're wrong," one coworker insisted. "They are here, and you must respect them."

Bob was not convinced until four weeks later when spirits showed up at his house.

A single father, Bob had moved into his apartment five months earlier with his two children, a seven-year-old daughter and five-year-old son.

As Bob faced serious health problems, his children alternated staying with his mother and sister, Christina, while Bob spent three weeks in the hospital. Even after his release, his children stayed with their grandmother and aunt, visiting him occasionally while he recuperated at the apartment.

One Friday night, Bob woke up with the feeling of a bad presence. His skin prickled with the undeniable impression that someone was watching him. But how could that be? It was the middle of the night. He was home alone with the doors locked. His children hadn't come over in the night, had they? Surely not.

Groggy from sleep, Bob sat up, eyes fixed on his blanket as they tried to focus. From the top edge of his vision, he noticed two figures standing near his bed. Ice water flushed through Bob's veins, and he shivered. This was not right. He didn't want to move, didn't want to look up, but after a few moments he realized he could only sit there for so long.

Reluctantly, he raised his eyes to see a strange, somber couple standing in front of him just a couple of feet from his bed. The woman wore a flowered short-sleeved dress that fell to her knees. A narrow belt circled her waist, and the rounded neckline beneath her chin had a small white collar tucked up against her throat.

It was hard to tell beneath his windbreaker jacket, but it looked as if the man had on a gray suit, white shirt, and narrow black tie.

They stood staring, unmoving, anxiety rising with each passing moment. Desperately wanting to escape, Bob wondered what would happen if he ran past the silent figures. Would they reach out a pale hand and grab him? Who were they, anyway? What were they doing in his house?

Slowly, Bob edged over to the side of the bed farthest away from the unwanted intruders. Then, as if sensing his fear, the couple backed slowly into the closet. When they reached the wall, they kept going until they disappeared.

Bob made a panicked dash out of the room, running as fast as his ailing body would let him until he reached his front door. Huddling against it, he debated about the wisdom of running out into the dark October night. It was cold out there. Whatever had been in his room hadn't hurt him. Drawing strength from being next to an exit, he told himself, *No, what you saw wasn't true. It didn't happen. No way. It was probably just the pain meds.*

Looking back over his shoulder and seeing no apparitions, Bob let himself fall into the rocking chair by the door. Not daring to return to his room, Bob stayed in the chair the rest of the night, getting what little sleep he could.

By Sunday night, after nearly convincing himself that what he saw was either part of a nightmare or a bad reaction to medication, Bob went back to sleeping in his room.

At 2:00 a.m., he was again woken by the presence. Heart pounding so hard it hurt, he sat up and saw that the couple was on the other side of the room, silently watching him.

This time he didn't wait, but slid out of the bed as far away from them as he could get. As he moved, so did they, backing up and disappearing through the wall.

Bob turned on the light and hurried into the living room as he had before, but was alarmed to find no safety there. He stared in dismay at the apparitions standing by the wall shared with his bedroom. Fear made him powerless in the face of his unwelcome visitors. They gazed back for a moment before slowly moving back through the wall and disappearing, as if he was not who they were looking for.

Okay, Bob thought, willing to believe that maybe spirits could come back after death, *One way or another, I've got to take care of this.*

As Bob began earnestly searching for another place to live, it occurred to him that he never saw the eerie couple when his children were home. The way the couple looked at him was as if they suspected him of hurting or abandoning his son and daughter. In his mind, he could almost hear them asking, "Where are your kids? Did you hurt them? You'd better not have. We miss them."

Bob shuddered in revulsion at the very idea. He was a loving father who would never abuse his children. He took except to any phantom that thought he would.

Summoning courage, Bob told some of his neighbors about his experiences. To his surprise, he learned that his apartment had once been part of an old mortuary, the abandoned building eventually carved into apartments.

Cold dread ran through Bob as he realized that the

two ridiculously large refrigerators in the back of the house had been used for keeping dead bodies before burial. He also discovered that his bedroom was where mortuary workers had prepped cadavers.

Bob stepped up his efforts to find a new place, but with Christmas right around the corner, people seemed more focused on the holidays than real estate.

That weekend, the children went to visit their mother, and Bob settled down to watch an evening movie to take his mind off things for awhile. He hadn't seen the unnatural couple for nearly two months, so when he got up to use the bathroom, he was startled by the sight of them standing at the end of the hallway. Their haunting gazes were full of silent accusations. The shock of their sudden reappearance sent Bob out to door and to his parents' house to spend the night.

That's the last time he saw the couple when he was alone.

Right after Christmas, Bob got the best gift ever - a house that he could buy for payments less than renting the haunted apartment. He got busy packing up his family's belongings even before the final papers were signed. Once he was cleared to move in, he was so eager to be free of the old mortuary and its ghostly residents that he worked packing boxes past dark. His children sat at the table eating a bedtime snack.

Stacking boxes next to the front window, Bob found himself moving the curtain to look outside, anticipating freedom from this creepy place. When he felt the urge to move the curtain again, he was suddenly afraid of what he might see. What if something outside was looking in at him? *No, Bob,* he told himself. *There's nothing there.*

With thoughts of a new house bolstering his courage, Bob took hold of the curtain and pulled it back. There was nothing outside the window, but just as he dropped the curtain back in place, he caught sight of a terrifying reflection inside his apartment. Icy chills shot through the top of head, standing his hair on end as he saw the phantom couple standing right behind his children. In horror, he watched the man put a hand on his little boy's shoulder. The couple's mouths moved as if they were talking, but Bob couldn't hear any sound.

Petrified for the safety of his children, Bob whirled around to protect them from the specters, but the couple had vanished.

I've got to get us out of this place now.

Bob took his daughter and son from the apartment that night and never brought them back.

Friends helped move furniture out while Bob shoved everything he could fit into his car. As hard as he tried, he couldn't get the last two boxes in, so he drove to the new place and unloaded what he had, feeling lighter with each box carried inside the welcoming new home. Even though he didn't want to go back, he had to get those last two boxes. With dread building higher the longer he put it off, he finally told himself to just hurry and get it over with.

Stopping in front of the apartment, he turned off his car and got out. Reluctantly stepping inside the apartment for the last time, he was struck with a cold sense of foreboding. The creepy feeling that someone was watching him followed him to the car with the first box. He dumped it on the back seat and dashed inside for the final box. Before he could pick it up, he was alarmed by a shadowy movement in the hallway.

Grabbing the box, he hurried out the door.

Balancing the box on his hip, he reached out to pull the door closed. That's when he saw the phantom couple come into the living room, their unblinking gaze fixed on him. With chills rolling up his arms to meet at the back of his neck, he pulled the door shut and tossed the box in his car.

As he slid behind the wheel and turned on the engine, Bob glanced back at the old mortuary one last time. His heart gave a little jolt when he saw the couple staring out at him through the window. He hit the gas and roared away.

"So now I know they're there," Bob says of spirits without bodies, "and I can respect that. I just don't want to run into them ever again."

When one of Bob's sister, Christina's, friends gushed about moving into the vacated apartment even before the contract was signed, she added a strange detail. Each night, she dreamed of people watching her.

Not wanting to dampen her friend's enthusiasm, and not knowing if she'd even be believed, Christina reluctantly told her friend of Bob's experience in that same apartment.

As soon as she heard the story, the new tenant called her boyfriend. "Don't you dare turn in that contract," she demanded. "The feeling I had in that place is real. We're moving."

January 10, 2015 was the last day Bob ever saw the unwelcome trespassers. He hasn't felt anything of a ghostly nature in his new house, and he's never gone back to the old one. He hasn't dared. He even avoids driving down the street where it sits at the roadside, waiting.

Who was the real trespasser? If the beings Bob saw were past patrons of the mortuary, hadn't they been in residence longer than he was? Why were they still there? Had they been prepped for burial, or had it been their child headed to the graveyard? Is that why Bob felt their dismay when his children were gone from home?

The Bathroom Across the Hall

Teenager Ellie Kreller was reading in the bedroom she shared with her sister, Allysa, when she was startled by three sharp knocks coming from the bathroom across the hall. Glancing up from her book, she wondered if her parents had come back home without her noticing. Hopefully they'd brought something good to eat. "Mom? Dad?"

No answer. Were they busy picking out all the treats from the grocery bags for themselves? They had been known to hide the good stuff.

Ellie got up and walked out into the hall, glancing through the open bathroom door. There was no one there. When she checked the rest of the house, she couldn't find anyone else home.

Hungry, she grabbed an apple and returned to her room to finish her book. She became so absorbed in reading that an hour passed before she again heard three loud knocks coming from the bathroom. Investigating again, she found the house as empty as before.

What was going on?

This time she called her parents and discovered they were on their way home, and only about five minutes away.

When they arrived, Ellie told them about the knocking. Her father said that sometimes pipes made a knocking sound.

The family had dinner together, and then Ellie and Allysa got ready for bed. After crawling under their blankets, they fell asleep until 2:00 a.m., when Ellie woke to the sound of whispering. Puzzled, she opened her eyes and raised her head to see what was going on. The only other living thing she saw in the room was Alyssa curled beneath her blankets, the slight, even rise and fall of her body indicating the rhythmic breathing of deep sleep.

Strange. If Allysa was asleep, who'd been whispering?

Too tired to wonder about it anymore, Ellie decided it must have been a remnant of her dream, and lay back down on her pillow.

Whispering voices filled her ears.

Ellie sat up quickly and stared at Allysa, trying to catch her mouth moving, but wasn't. Alyssa didn't sigh, roll over, giggle, or stick her tongue out at Ellie. She appeared to be genuinely asleep.

Suddenly, Ellie noticed movement out of the corner of her eye. Turning toward the open door, she stared in horror at a ghostly black figure gliding past the doorway.

Frozen with fear, she sat rigid for a few moments. *What was that thing?*

It didn't move like a walking person, but instead seemed to float, skimming just above the ground. Where was it going? Worse yet, what if it came back?

Heart hammering with renewed fear at the thought of seeing that terrible apparition again, Ellie slowly laid back down on her pillow, pulled her covers up as carefully as she could to avoid any unwanted attention, and pretended to sleep.

In spite of her intense fear, her exhausted body eventually fell asleep, and was relieved to open her eyes in the quiet morning light.

What caused the urgent knocking across the hall? Was it from old bathroom pipes? Or had some spirits stopped by to use the toilet? Were some of them taking too long? Was there ghostly gossip about the ones who were hogging the bathroom? Ellie may never know. All she knows is that since that night, she hasn't heard or seen any more strange things in the bathroom across the hall.

Fred

Nikysha Rostron suddenly woke up in the middle of the night, unnerved by her unfamiliar surroundings until she remembered that she was staying at her aunt's house.

Something moved beside her. She nearly screamed until she recognized her cousin getting up and walking toward the door. In a voice sharp with fear, Nikysha asked, "What are you doing?"

Her cousin scowled at her and mumbled, "Getting a drink of water." Nikysha lay back and stared up into the darkness, wondering why she felt so restless.

All of a sudden, her cousin dashed back into the room, dove into bed, and flung the covers over her head. "What are you doing?" Nikysha whispered.

"Hiding from Fred."

"Fred who?"

"Fred the ghost."

Nikysha felt a cold finger slide down her back. "What are you talking about?"

Her cousin's eyes peeked out from under the blanket. "When I went to get a drink, the popcorn machine was going."

"So? Your mom likes popcorn."

"There was no one beside it," her cousin insisted. "And when I moved closer to check it out, Fred threw popcorn in my face."

"You're kidding," Nikysha declared, hoping it was true.

Her cousin shook her head. "No. Fred's thrown stuff before, like Santa Claus decorations. When we first moved in and were fixing things up, Fred picked up a hammer and started hammering along with us. He's even turned on the blender in the middle of the night."

"So, who is Fred? Or who was he?" Nikysha whispered as the scent of fresh popcorn drifted through the doorway. "How do you even know the ghost is a boy? Have you seen him?"

"No." Her cousin bunched the blankets up against her chin. "It's just that the next door neighbors had a really bad car wreck just before we moved here. Their little eight year old boy died. It was so sad. Fred does things that are just like a little kid, so we figure he's the ghost of that boy."

If the strange happenings were due to Fred, why did he hang out at the neighbor's house instead of his own? Had the previous owners given him cookies? Or, like any curious eight-year-old, did he go back and forth from house to house, depending on which place looked most interesting at the time?

The Kitchen Ghost

Like most eleven-year-olds, Luis Santoyo was excited to spend the night at his friend's house. He walked over beneath a sky filled with gray rain clouds. The rising wind pushed him along until he reached the front door, where he was let in out of the brewing storm.

As expected, the boys stayed up late, talking, eating, and watching TV. Around midnight, his friend's mother finally told them it was time to settle down and sleep.

Everything was turned off, making Luis suddenly aware of the branches whipping around outside and the wind howling around the corners of the house. Luis settled onto the couch that faced the open doorway to the kitchen and closed his eyes, but the noise of the storm made it hard to relax. He kept shifting on the unfamiliar bed, opening and closing his eyes as he tried to get comfortable enough to fall asleep.

When he opened his eyes again around 2:00 am, he was shocked to see a dark figure standing in the kitchen doorway, facing him. It wasn't anyone he recognized, and his fear grew as he realized that he could see right through the motionless figure cloaked in black. His horror reached the point of making him tremble when the apparition raised a hand and beckoned for Luis to come closer.

No way. He wasn't going anywhere near it.

Not daring to get up, Luis turned over on the couch to face the window, putting his back to the thing in the doorway, hoping that if he didn't look at it, it would go away.

Startled by a sudden bolt of lightning that made the night bright as day for an instant, Luis was shocked to see the same semi-transparent figure walking away from the house and moving right through a fence around the yard as if it weren't even there.

Impossible. How had it gone from right behind him to outside in such a short time, unless there were two of them.

Luis glanced fearfully over his shoulder. The doorway was empty, but apparently the kitchen was not. Footsteps sounded, slow and measured, in the deep darkness following the lightning flash. Rattling sounds came from the inky kitchen blackness. A drawer? Pans? Knives? Luis didn't know, and he wasn't going to check. No one in the household would move around the kitchen in pitch blackness. Had the ghost circled back as quickly as it left, entering by an outside door, or through the wall? Something told Luis that whatever was out there did not belong to his friend's family, at least it wasn't anything alive.

Luis hunkered down on the couch, pressing himself into the space between the cushions as far as he could, and tried to drop back into the safe oblivion of sleep.

As soon as the household began moving around in the morning, Luis told them what he'd seen.

They didn't believe him.

Later, his friend got him alone and confessed that he'd also seen a ghost in the house. His sister confirmed that she'd seen it, too, both describing the ghost with a slash across its middle, exposing the stomach cavity, offering a graphic view of glistening intestines.

Luis could have seen a different ghost, or the same one without the black cloak.

Was the apparition inviting Luis to join it for a late-night snack? Or did it want Luis to help it cut something up, because it had once been too careless with a knife?

Ghostly Guardian

Thirteen-year-old Peter felt practically grown-up when his parents said he could stay home with his 16-year-old brother, Jimmy, while they were out of town. Best of all, Mom and Dad packed a suitcase for Peter's little sister, Debbie, and took her with them to Colorado, leaving Peter and Jimmy the run of their 2-story house. With Jimmy's new driver's license, they were invincible.

As masters of their own fate, they decided to watch TV in the middle of the day with plenty of chips, soda, and ice cream at hand. Settling themselves on the couch beneath the second-story railing looking over the TV room, they clicked through channels, considering some shows that their parents didn't like. Not having Debbie complaining or grabbing for the remote control was great, until the pillow appeared.

Choosing a questionable action movie, they were riveted to the screen as the plot built to such a crescendo that Peter wondered how the hero could possibly get out alive, when something pink and round sailed over the upstairs railing, bounced against the floor, and rolled to a stop.

Peter jumped, with the startling impression that a human head had come crashing down. Staring down in disbelief, he recognized his sister's pig-shaped pillow. Glancing at Jimmy, he saw his brother's eyes wide with surprise. "Who threw that?" Jimmy demanded.

"How should I know?" Peter answered. "Didn't Mom and Dad take Debbie with them?"

"Of course." Jimmy's reply was tense with fear. "Who've you got hiding up there?"

Shocked at his accusation, Peter answered, "No one!"

Jimmy's eyes narrowed. "Let's just go see, why don't we?"

Peter reluctantly followed his brother up the stairs. Was Jimmy playing a trick on him? Did he have a friend hiding up here who planned to jump out and scare him half to death?

With cautions steps, the brothers examined every upstairs room, every closet, and under under every bed.

No one was there.

The second story windows were too high to get down from without a ladder, and there were no ladders.

Jimmy looked just as scared as Peter felt.

The brothers slowly returned to the TV room where the movie still played, but the suspense no longer gripped Peter as it had before.

Jimmy picked up the remote control. Before he could click the TV off, his hand froze in mid-air as a dark shadow crossed in front of the screen. "Did you see that?" he whispered.

Peter swallowed twice before he could force out the single word, "Yeah."

"What was it?"

"Don't know."

The television screen went blank.

Click, clack, click.

Peter's head swiveled toward the hallway, listening to the sound coming from the kitchen, a sound eerily like someone repeatedly pushing the button at the end of a pen.

Clickety, clack, click, clack.

Peter jumped at the light sound of metal clicking beside him. Whipping his head around, he saw Jimmy flipping through the key ring he carried in his pocket, singling out the car key. "Let's go," he whispered.

He didn't have to tell Peter twice.

The boys ran outside, jumped in the car, and escaped to the family farm.

When their parents returned and heard about the strange events, they just laughed them off.

Was it because they didn't believe their boys? Or was it because they had somehow employed an other-worldly guardian to make sure the boys followed the house rules in their absence?

An Abundance of Ghosts

Cassi Hender and her family seem to have encountered more spirits than most people brush up against in a lifetime. For example, on the morning of a family dental appointment, while Cassi brushed her teeth, she saw something very unusual from the corner of her eye. A boy just over four feet tall, wearing pajama pants and a shirt, stood watching her.

His thick, dark hair hung over a strangely pale face, framing beautiful brown eyes staring at Cassi as if longing for a hug. When he smiled, Cassi turned his way, but could no longer see him when she looked directly at the spot where he'd been.

She still doesn't know who he was. Perhaps in some long ago night, he'd brushed his teeth and missed a good night hug that he was still hoping to collect on.

On another occasion, Cassi knelt with her family for evening prayers. She admits to being a peeker, so she was the only one who saw her grandmother's ghost walk into the living room. Glad to see her, comfort washed over Cassi as she watched Grandma sit down in an empty chair, close her eyes, and bow her head as the prayer was said. She was gone when the prayer ended.

Not to be left out, Grandpa's ghost stood in the doorway when Cassi's mom tried to walk into the kitchen. Since Grandpa was a really big guy, Cassi's mother felt as if she'd run into a brick wall. She heard her father's laughter and felt his words in her mind, "Would you really walk into me if you saw me?"

In spite of feeling her father's jovial presence, or maybe because of it, Cassi's mom decided to move the family into an old pink mansion. It had no fairy tale ending.

Cassi and her siblings couldn't make themselves go downstairs alone after dark because of feelings that some being lurked down there. After the sun went down, they always crept down the steps to the bathroom with a buddy, then ran back up the staircase as soon as they could.

This overly-cautious behavior was validated when Cassi overheard her mother saying that she'd seen a grossly weird yellow-colored demon with black eyes that winked at her, giving her the creepy shivers.

Could it have been associated with the person who'd died in the house? Cassi saw the gray man after she played on a rope hanging from a willow tree. She and her siblings spent a fair amount of time swinging on the long rope in the yard. When they were done, they left it trailing on the ground and went inside.

In the morning, the children looked out the window to see a ghostly gray stranger standing next to the willow tree, staring at the rope. Then, with a sudden sense of dread, the children watched him swing his dead gaze over to at them and stare through the window. They stumbled over one another in their haste to back away from the glass.

Once he was gone, they went outside to see the rope neatly coiled beneath the tree. Each time the children left the rope trailing on the ground, they'd return to find it neatly coiled.

When Cassi saw the ghost repeatedly, she told her father, "Our house is haunted."

"I know," he said, "I'm trying to fix it."

The remedy ended up being a move to another house, where the rope man didn't follow.

There was an even more frightening experience awaiting them.

Cassi's teenage brother, who was struggling with addictions, often stayed up all night. One morning he was in the kitchen at 3:00 am when he saw a black figure walk through the living room and up the stairs. This faceless being was no one in his family. It felt demonic, and freaked him out so much that he told Cassi it was there because he wasn't making very good choices about his life.

Cassi believes that something strange has attached itself to her family, because her aunt's house has been the site of unexplained happenings. Cassi, along with several family members including her brother, mother, grandma, aunt and uncle, have had weird experiences with a feeling that's not exactly possession, but definitely not normal, that's come over them while lying in bed. Lights flash and their ears ring as they can't move.

in their eyes and they have ringing in their ears. Worst of all, they can't move.

Why is it that some people and particular families seem to attract ghosts? And what is it about Cassi's family that has made it a wide-flung ghost magnet?

Ghostly Flirtation

Marijah Fraser hiked her backpack up on her shoulders and headed for the imposing high school building, hoping for a good freshman year.

It would have been better without the ghost.

She first noticed something wrong when she walked down the school hall and suddenly felt a heaviness on her back as if someone had tugged on her backpack. Turning around, she was astonished to see that no one was close enough to have touched her pack, let alone pull on it. Confused, Marijah turned around and headed for class.

That wasn't the only time she felt the ghostly tug. Her pack was pulled several times, both when she was alone and while in the midst of other students. She didn't like it, but how could she stop it? And where was it coming from? The only explanation that made sense to Marijah was that a ghost roamed the school halls.

Then it followed her home.

Walking toward her house on a scarcely traveled road, Marijah felt the unmistakable slip of her shoe sliding off her heel, just as if one of her friends had intentionally stepped on the back of her shoe to pull it off. Marijah walked right out of her shoe before she could stop her forward momentum, then stopped still while a sudden coldness crept over her. Even before turning around, she had the eerie feeling that she wouldn't see anyone. Glancing back, she saw it was true. No one was there.

Feeling more scared than she ever had while at school, Marijah stuck her foot back in her shoe and ran the rest of the way home.

After several more incidents of feeling the ghost tug on her pack and step on her heels, it gradually stopped. Mariah doesn't know why.

Her friend, Kayona, has an idea. Without naming names, Kayona says that another girl has been bothered with the same kind of ghostly shenanigans.

Could the ghost be a former high school student who passed on before he ever graduated, so he visits the school halls, still playing the field?

Short One Player

The day Mackenzie Wade ate her lunch in the school locker room was a day she wanted to be alone, but it seemed as if ghosts wanted to keep her company.

Settled on a backless bench with a sandwich in her hand, Mackenzie heard a locker open and shut. Strange. When she'd come in, she was sure she was alone. She waited for footsteps to signal the departure of her unwanted lunch partner, but there was no sound. After a long moment, she tentatively called, "Hello?"

Silence.

Prickles rising on the back of her neck, Mackenzie swallowed the dryness from her throat and called a little louder, "Hello? Is anybody there?"

Silence.

Mackenzie wondered if her friend Ashley, who sometimes came in the locker room to eat lunch with her, had snuck in to give her a scare. Well, she'd stop that right now. Mackenzie quietly walked around the bank of lockers, but found no one. Checking the bathroom, looking in the showers, and pushing open the doors on the stalls revealed nothing. There was nowhere else to search.

With a sudden frightening sense that something bad was going to happen to her, Mackenzie rushed from the locker room before the bell rang, nearly running over Ashley.

"What's wrong?" Ashley asked.

"I think there's a ghost in there," Mackenzie answered, pointing a shaking finger at the locker room door.

"Show me."

Bolstered by Ashley's presence, Mackenzie crept back into the deathly silent locker room. Finding no evidence of ghostly activity, Ashley turned with a smirk and said, "Good one, Kenz."

"I really heard a locker slam shut!"

"You probably fell asleep and dreamed it."

"I was awake!"

"Whatever."

When the bell rang, the girls went their separate ways.

As she thought over her experience, Mackenzie's curiosity grew bigger than her fear. Since she preferred eating lunch alone in the locker room, she decided to go there again, not knowing if anything else would happen.

It turned out that a couple of times a week, she heard noises coming from different areas in the room when she was alone. More lockers opened and shut with no one by them, and she also heard what sounded like people's clothing rubbing against the lockers as if jostling for position or to reach around each other. It never happened when Ashley was there. Only when Mackenzie was alone.

Could it be that a phantom team is hoping to recruit Mackenzie to join them?

Running in the Halls

When Darci Barker was a high school freshman, she took advantage of the evening math tutoring offered at school. Walking into the dimly lit building with night creeping over the lawn made her uneasy. Entering the brightly lit classroom made her feel better, until she overheard some of the seniors talking about hearing running footsteps in the halls. When they checked on the sound, no one was there.

Seeing her watching them with wide eyes, they explained that even when they hurried to the end of the hallway that turned into the darkened halls spreading out to the rest of the empty school building, they didn't see anyone. They didn't see how flesh and blood people could run that fast. It had to be ghosts.

Some math teachers who stay late to help students say the running footfalls are from young children who escaped their parents who've come to school to watch ball games in the gym.

While Darci admits that part of her fear of entering the darkened high school could stem from the stories told her by the upperclassmen, all she knows is that she's glad the math tutor rooms in the echoing, mostly empty hallways are close to the exit doors.

Are the running footfalls from flesh and blood children? Or do they come from disembodied former math students running away from extra schoolwork?

Little Boy Ghost

Yutauna's father works in a coal mine with a little boy named Charlie. Charlie's not authorized to be there, since by modern standards he's too young to be in the mines, but he won't leave.

The story is that he was killed in a mine explosion many years ago, before child labor laws would have kept him home eating warm bread and honey under his fond mother's gaze. Instead, he was deep in the mine, crawling through spaces too small for a grown man to go, placing explosives as long as his arm in preparation of widening the passage to man-size. But a fatal, unplanned explosion ensured that Charlie would never grow to be a man.

Charlie generally stays in the mine, doing his best to warn the miners of danger by whistling. They occasionally hear his quick footsteps, but never see him.

There are times when he finds a worker he particularly likes. Maybe he's tempted by whatever's in the miner's lunch box. Maybe Charlie hears him talk about his children, and is intrigued by mention of a nine-year-old, just like him. For whatever reason, he sometimes follows a worker home and stays for a day or two, running in the halls at night and whistling. But before long, he's back to his real home, in the mine.

What's keeping Charlie here? Does he want another chance to place the dynamite? Does he know how to fix it now so that it won't blow him and his co-workers into the next life?

Ghostly Music

Nikysha Rostron's friends Jentrie and Marijah were at her house getting a snack in the kitchen when all of a sudden they heard music playing. That was strange, because Nikysha thought they were home alone. "Mom?" she called.

No answer.

"It sounds like it's coming from upstairs," Jentrie said.

The three friends trooped up the stairs, but as soon as they reached the upper landing, the musical strains floated up to them from where they'd just been standing at the bottom of the staircase. Pointing, Marijah said, "Now it sounds like the music's playing down there."

Hurrying down to locate the elusive music source, the unmistakable measures of music seemed to reverberate along the upstairs hallways again. It didn't matter if the girls were upstairs or down, the music seemed to move in the opposite direction,

Then, looking out the window at an old elementary school, Marijah sighed and said, "Now it sounds like it's coming from over there."

Perhaps it came from was a budding musician, like the unseen ones heard at the middle school when Jentrie Allsop and her violin-playing friends Marijah Fraser, Alyssa White, and Mackenzie Wade stayed after school in the orchestra room one day.

"We turned off all the lights," Jentrie admits with a shiver. "Then we sat in the corner and waited. Then all the music stands started moving, sliding a little way across the floor and making noise like *skr...skr...skr....*"

It was too dark to actually see the movement, but the girls clung together as the shimmying music stands seemed to draw closer. Jentrie's eyes started watering, and her body shook from the creepy activity.

At last the girls jumped up, screaming, and ran to the door, nearly tripping over one another's feet. One of them fumbled for the handle, desperately trying to open it, but it wouldn't budge. Other hands grasped hers, squeezing and pinching in panicked attempts to turn the knob. "Let us out!" Jentrie screamed in the dark, pounding on the door.

"We're going to die!" Marijah wailed.

At last, the door gave way under the frightened girls' pounding, and they nearly crashed into the orchestra teacher, Mrs. Murray. Eyes wide, she stepped back to keep from falling over as the frightened girls spilled out into the hallway, claiming that the music stands were moving on their own.

Mrs. Murray told the girls that the girls should go home as soon as schoo let out.

Not long afterward, the girls invited Jaynie Ivie to sit in the orchestra room after school hours to listen to the haunted music stands. That time, the stands were still and quiet. Jaynie was not impressed.

"We did it ten times and they only moved, like, three times," Jentrie admitted.

Where was the music source in the house? Was it from from some long-ago teenager who avoided anyone who might tell him or her to turn the music down?

Why did the music stands move on their own? Were there ghostly players taking the time after school to practice, adjusting the stands to the right position? Or were the stands themselves haunted by the music they've absorbed through the years?

Kevin

"Bye, Mom," Jentrie called, "I'm going to Abby's." Jentrie stuffed a cookie in her mouth and hurried out the door. As the youngest in her family, Jentrie liked helping Abby babysit her little sister, Claire. It was especially fun when Claire was put to bed, leaving the older girls alone to eat popcorn and talk about boys.

If Jentrie had known a ghost was going to help babysit that night, she may have stayed home.

Abby's parents welcomed her, then fussed with instructions about locking doors, not opening for strangers, not staying up late, and brushing teeth. They finally went out the door, smiling and gripping each other's hands like teenagers.

Abby popped corn, and Claire snuggled on the couch between the two friends with her stuffed rabbit on her lap while they watched "Ella Enchanted." When the show was over, Abby announced, "Time for bed."

Claire looked up at her with wide eyes. "One more show?"

"No way," Abby replied. "Then you might be awake when Mom and Dad get home."

"But I'm scared." Claire clutched her bunny close.

"Of what?"

Claire ducked her head so that her next words were muffled. "The guy."

"Is he cute?" Jentrie joked.

She felt bad for her careless words when Claire raised her head, showing a tear streaking down her baby-soft cheek. "I can't see his face," Claire said with a little shiver, "but he turns off my light."

"Maybe the bulb is burned out," Abby said. "Let's go check."

Upstairs, Claire's star-shaped night light suffused her room with a warm glow through the darkness. "See?" Abby said. "It's working fine."

Claire gave it a forlorn glance.

"Let's get your teeth brushed, then Jentrie can tell you a story," Abby said, giving Claire's hand a tug.

"Me?" Jentrie asked.

"Sure," Abby said with a grin. "Something about unicorns and sparkles would be good."

Once Claire was settled among her stuffed animal army with her bunny in her arms, Jentrie sat beside the bed and started in on a rambling tale about unicorns flying over islands and a hula girl named Claire throwing stars up in the sky for them to catch. She noticed Abby slip from the room, but since Claire was so quiet she might be falling asleep, Jentrie didn't dare stop her story.

A few minutes later, Abby was at the door, beckoning furiously to Jentrie. Jentrie stood and tiptoed toward her. Claire didn't make a sound. Good. She must be asleep.

Jentrie nearly stumbled in the sudden dark when Claire's night light flickered off. Almost immediately, it flicked on again. Jentrie made it out the door and pulled it closed behind her.

Abby gripped her arm and steered her toward the top of the stairs. Pointing down at the brightly lit landing, she whispered, "I was going down to get my phone, but the lights downstairs keep turning on and off."

"Maybe your parents are home."

"I don't think so." Abby bit her lip. "I'd have heard the car. They're not talking. I'm pretty sure no one's here but us...at least they shouldn't be. Mom locked all the doors before she left, and I checked the front door after they went out."

A cold ripple traveled across Jentrie's shoulders. "What was that thing Claire said about a guy turning off lights?"

Abby shrugged. "She started saying that a couple of days ago. I thought she must have seen part of a scary TV show or something."

"What if it wasn't a TV show?" Jentrie asked, her heart thudding with excitement. "What if it's real?"

Abby gave an un-ladylike snort. "Don't you think that if some guy were in here turning lights on and off, we'd see him?"

Jentrie leaned closer. Through a mischievous grin, she said, "Not if he's a ghost."

Abby went still. "There's no such things as ghosts."

The lights downstairs flicked off, plunging the teenagers into darkness. Abby shrieked and clutched Jentrie. "Maybe I should call the police," she gasped.

"That would be weird if it's just something wrong with your electricity," Jentrie said. If it really is a ghost, we should call him 'Kevin'."

Abby snorted. "As in Kevin Jones, Senior class hunk?"

"Not necessarily," Jentrie said. "There are lots of guys named Kevin."

"Whatever."

Jentrie sat down on the top step, pulling Abby

down beside her as they faced the darkened stairs. "Kevin?" she called, "if you're real, then please turn the lights on."

A bright beam of yellow shot up the stairs as the lights suddenly flicked on. Abby squealed and covered her face with her hands, while Jentrie blinked in surprise at the sudden brightness.

Neither girl went downstairs until Abby's parents got home. When they told them what had happened, Abby's dad checked the breaker box, but didn't find anything wrong. He said if it kept being a problem, he'd have it checked.

It didn't happen again.

Why did the lights go on and off by themselves? Was there some kind of temporary electrical problem? Or was there a spirit in the house? Once Kevin got a name, was he playfully teasing Jentrie and Abby, trying to lure them downstairs?

Halloween in the Cemetery

Jentrie Allsop's mother, Carrie, is the kind of mom who understands teenage girls. She goes along with their shenanigans, including willingness to drive her 13-year-old daughter and two of her friends, Mckayla and Reggie, to the cemetery on Halloween night in 2011.

The old cemetery, which welcomed its first underground resident in the horse and buggy days of the mid-1800's, bristles with tall headstones and several funeral pillars cracked with age. Following a long line of ancient pine trees spreading their limbs to the edge of Highway 89 which borders the cemetery, new plots are filled as local folks pass on.

After leaving Carrie waiting in the car, the friends walked around the shadowy headstones. Darting among the few trees scattered in the midst of cemetery paths wide enough for a car to drive along, they shouted, "Boo!" to each other. Then they tried to get the angel statue to turn her head. The legend is that if someone walks around the statue three times at night, then the angel will turn her cold stone eyes toward you, and maybe cry a tear or two.

When that didn't happen, the three friends decided to scare Carrie. Working their way back to the car from behind, they crept through the dark from tree to tree, planning to jump out at the last moment and scare her through the car window.

It didn't work out as planned. Before they got close to the car, the three friends spotted a strange human shape running toward them through the screen of pines from the opposite side of the row of trees, dark in the shadows. They couldn't make out any features on its face or hear any sound of footsteps, even as the entity drew rapidly nearer.

Terrified, the teens ran as fast as they could away from the eerie figure toward the far side of the cemetery, abandoning their plan to scare Mom. When they finally turned to look behind them, they couldn't see whatever had chased them anymore. Instead, they faced a wide expanse of cold headstones thrown in sharp relief by their own dark shadows.

When the friends huddled together to make their awkward way to Carrie's car. Carrie raised her seat from its reclined position and rolled down her window. Before she could ask if they were ready to go, Jentrie blurted, "Mom, was that you?"

Carrie looked startled. "Was what me?"

"Chasing us through the trees."

"What?" Carrie's honest surprise would be hard to fake. "Why would I do that? I've been sleeping." Carrie looked out her window, her gaze suddenly suspicious. "Who else is here? I don't see anyone."

To her credit, Carrie's eyes did look sleepy. Besides, Jentrie couldn't imagine her mother running just for fun. She certainly couldn't run as fast as the dark figure had.

So who...or what...chased the teens through the cemetery? Was it someone else on the streets planning a Halloween scare? Where did the figure go when the frightened teens ran across the cemetery? Could the dark thing have been something from another world? Could it have been a cemetery spirit from the horse and buggy days, returning home from a Halloween romp?

Ghostly Corpse

When sixteen-year-old Jaynie Ivie's family moved to an old house in Manti, Utah, they thought the recently remodeled home was empty, until Jaynie's 22-year-old sister, Jenn, saw someone else there.

Late on the same day they moved in, Jenn admitted to Jaynie that she'd been feeling creepy all day. Just as she finished speaking, the lights in the big house dimmed. Alarmed, Jaynie sat bolt upright and glanced over her shoulder. Even thought she didn't see anything unusual, something made her skin go cold.

Jenn shivered. "I've got to go to the bathroom." She walked down the hall and Jaynie heard the bathroom door open and close.

Finding herself alone, Jaynie sat right where she was, unwilling to move until her sister came back. There was no reason for it, except that something felt strange. Being alone in the house felt weird.

Clasping her cold hands between her knees, Jaynie couldn't help remembering her parents telling her about a friend of theirs who, at nineteen years old, thought it would be funny to summon the devil. Leaving her friends in the living room, she went into the basement by herself where she chanted an incantation meant to call the devil to her.

When her friends went looking, they found her passed out on the basement floor. After they managed to bring her around, she stared at them with weird, round eyes and claimed she'd seen the devil. From that day until she died just twelve brief years later, the woman was either afraid of everything or acted possessed.

When Jaynie first met her, the woman stared through wide, desperate eyes, greeting Jaynie with a mouth that opened too big, speaking in a strange voice that made Jaynie uneasy.

When she heard the bathroom door open again, Jaynie started to relax. Then, as if her sister had paused just long enough to take a breath, Jenn screamed.

A jolt of fear darted through Jaynie, leaving a trail of gooseflesh in its wake. Jenn burst out of the hallway, pounding toward the front door, yanking it open and dashing outside, hair streaming behind her.

Jaynie gazed at the open doorway for a startled

second before racing after her sister. "What's wrong?" she called when she saw Jenn standing on the sidewalk, gasping, wide eyes staring at the house through rising tears.

"When I walked out of the bathroom, I turned around and glanced back." Trembling, Jenn put her hands to her face and let out a sob.

"What happened?" Jaynie asked, rubbing her sister's back.

Through her hands, Jenn mumbled, "I saw a ghost in there," she took a shuddering breath, "a ghost standing over a dead body."

Jaynie shivered from head to toe. Voice quivering, she asked, "Is the dead body still there?"

Her sister turned toward her with haunted eyes. "It was a ghost body."

When Jenn refused to go back inside, Jaynie got her parents. Mom and Dad finally talked their older daughter into returning to the house.

Jenn won't stay alone in the house. It's a good thing there are two bathrooms, because Jenn refuses to go near the haunted one.

Jaynie's never seen anything in the house, but she's felt something disturbing. "If you're alone, it's weird," she says. "It's a big house, and sometimes it's creepy if you're by yourself."

Her sister's experience made her wonder — if there's a ghost in the bathroom, who is it? And who is the "dead" ghost? Did someone slip in the claw foot tub long ago and have a fatal accident? Or was someone badly burned and dragged to the bathroom for a cooling water treatment that failed? Perhaps the sink or tub was used to catch the blood of a bleeding victim. Had someone died in the house before bathrooms were invented, or was the only glimpse of an old-time murder given to a terrified young woman a hundred years too late?

Ghost Sense

When nine-year-old Rachel moved to Hobbes, New Mexico, her new home made her very uneasy. She discovered she wasn't the only one who felt apprehensive when her 14-year-old brother, Paul, told her that he'd seen a strange little black-haired girl in a white dress standing in their backyard. When he glanced away and back again, the girl had vanished. Since they both believed something strange was going on, Rachel agreed to help Paul conduct an experiment. She was to walk through the house with her brother and tell him how she felt in each room.

"We started in the front lobby and I felt fine," Rachel says. "Then we went into my room and I had this horrible feeling like something was there. Next we went into my brother's room and there was an even more overwhelming feeling of darkness, but I felt most fearful in our parents' room."

It wasn't until two years later, after their family moved out of the house, that Rachel and Paul looked up its history. "We discovered there had been a murder committed there," Rachel said. "It happened in my brother's closet."

Since then, Rachel's ability to feel spirits has never gone away. "I'm sensitive to spirits that have some kind of impact on me, but I don't sense spirits that are interacting with other people," she explains. "You either believe in ghosts and spirits or you don't.

If you've had an experience, you usually believe. If you haven't, you probably don't."

While Rachel sees her whole family as being sensitive to spirits, her brother has a particular affinity to see things, while Rachel feels and hears them.

In 2012, Rachel was nearly eighteen years old when she had a personal ghostly experience in Utah. "I felt something following me all the time," Rachel explains. "I was so scared. I'm not crazy. I can tell if there's a spirit around me, and this one never left me alone. I felt this thing most strongly downstairs. The only place I felt safe was in my room or in my bed, but even there I couldn't escape a constantly dark, overwhelming feeling that filled me with anxiety."

One day while walking through the living room past an Xbox on the console, she felt the thing behind her so intensely that she ran to her room too fast to pull the door closed.

That's when the Xbox lid made the same scratchy sound it did whenever Rachel's cat jumped up on it. Thinking she'd bring her cat in her room to comfort her, Rachel crept into the living room, but couldn't see her cat anywhere. Confused, she moved closer to the Xbox, still searching. Standing right in front of the console, Rachel heard the sound repeated with no living thing in sight, which terrified her into running back to her room.

When Rachel's friend, Heather, had a sleepover at Rachel's house, she encountered a huge 6' 3" tall guy in the hallway. In spite of his intimidating appearance, the spiritually sensitive Heather demanded, "What are you doing here?"

"I'm here to destroy this family."

"No, you're not."

"Yes I am. Rachel's made a contract with me.

And after this one, I'm going to move on to the next family, and the next, and the next."

When Rachel heard about Heather's encounter, she thought about what she was doing with her life. Recognizing she was doing things that she knew were wrong, she realized she couldn't blame her behavior on her upbringing, like her brother did. "He lives a very weird lifestyle," Rachel says. "He blames his disbelief in God on our mother." Having divorced their pornography-addicted father when Rachel was four, her mother married a religious, yet abusive man. In spite of his actions, their mother would not leave him, believing their marriage was necessary to her salvation. She didn't know that she could attain her heart's desire whether she had a husband or not.

After Rachel's mother died, her brother partied and did a lot of things he shouldn't do. Not wanting to be in the same situation, Rachel changed her behavior, and was relieved that she never felt that awful spirit again.

When Rachel's family left town, Rachel moved to Heather's house. One night she returned home at 10:30 pm and found herself alone. Even after climbing into bed in her downstairs room, she was too restless to fall sleep.

Then, to her horror, she heard two male voices whispering outside her door. She couldn't make out what they said, but their speech didn't sound like anything of this world. Frightened, she listened harder, hoping to hear Heather, her brother, Jackson, or their father return home. They always came in loud and laughing, which would be a welcome disturbance, especially if they scared away whatever was lurking outside her door. She heard footfalls on the floor overhead, but no voices or laughter, so she decided that whatever was walking around up there was not her friend.

Suddenly, Rachel was washed with paralyzing sorrow so deep and agonizing that she feared for her life. Loneliness squeezed her so hard that she trembled, while hot tears rolled down her face.

Thankfully, Heather returned soon afterward. Rachel summoned her with a quavering voice. Heather wasn't surprised by Rachel's experience. When Heather said, "That happens all the time down here," Rachel pulled a blanket and pillow off the bed and hurried upstairs to sleep on the couch.

That didn't turn out to be any safer, because one dark night, she heard quiet footfalls across the floor. Then she sensed the presence of a tall, scrawny man bending over the couch to stare at her, his breath puffing against her cheek. She immediately tensed, her heart racing with fear, but at the same time, she perceived the loneliness of his sad spirit.

Jackson said he'd seen that same spirit huddled in a corner. No one knew why the thin, lonely being hadn't shied away from Rachel.

Rachel may have gotten some of her ability to sense spirits from her Grandma, who spoke to her dead daughter and brother, Tina and Donny, as she lay dying. Grandma stopped talking to her ghostly visitors long enough to announce, "Tina's doing most of the talking." As soon as Grandma's other daughter walked into the room, Grandma smiled at her, then passed away.

Why did young Rachel feel the most uneasy in her parents' room if the murder happened in her brother's closet? Had the killer lived in the parents' room?

What was the huge being that wanted to destroy Rachel's family? Was it something Rachel had summoned because of the way she was living?

What whispered outside her bedroom door when she was alone? Was it the cowardly ghost? If so, who or what was he talking to? Could he have been acting as sentry to keep other spirits away from Rachel? Why was he brave enough to take a closer look at Rachel while she slept? Did she remind him of someone he once knew?

Did Grandma hang on for a final earthly glimpse of her mortal daughter before taking the hands of her dead daughter and brother to move into the next life?

Track Ghost

Kenna Hill saw the stranger while walking around the school track with her friends during weight lifting class. Even though they weren't walking fast, Kenna, Stephanie, and Morgan reassured themselves it counted as exercise. The thing is, their heart rates didn't go up until they glimpsed a man dressed all in white standing by the hurdles.

At first, nothing seemed out of the ordinary, since track coaches often inspected the equipment both before and after a meet. But once they noticed him, they glanced down at the track and took another step. Then, realizing that this man was unfamiliar, Kenna looked up again.

The man was gone.

"Where'd he go?" Kenna asked, shading her eyes to look out across the field.

"Who?" Stephanie asked.

"That guy in white," Kenna said, looking over at Morgan, whose eyes were unnaturally wide.

"Didn't you see him?" Morgan asked.

"What? The guy in white shorts?" Stephanie studied the hurdles with a puzzled look.

"Yeah," Morgan said, gripping Stephanie's arm. "He was there, and now he disappeared, like a ghost."

Stephanie pulled back a little, asking, "Are you okay?"

Morgan's voice trembled. "I'm so scared, I might pee my pants."

Stephanie laughed. "He was only fixing something on the hurdles. He was there just a second ago, so he must be around here somewhere."

"He's not," Kenna said, shaking her head. "He was there, and now he's just…gone. There's no way he could have gotten away that fast without us seeing him."

Morgan gripped Kenna's arm as if it were a shield. "Everything he had on was white - clothes, shoes, even his hair. He has to be a ghost. I'm getting out of here."

Stephanie and Kenna didn't argue, but hurried after Morgan, casting glances around them as they left. None of them caught another glimpse of the stranger in white.

All the girls insist he could not have been flesh and blood, because he disappeared too quickly. None of them recognized him, so who was he? Was he a former coach? Or an athlete who met his end through an unfortunate equipment malfunction on the field, and came back to make sure the hurdles wouldn't trip anyone else up so they became a ghost like him?

The Ephraim Co-op Ghost

The building's historical significance goes back to 1871 when it was built as one of the first ZCMI (Zion's Cooperative Mercantile Institution) stores in Utah Territory. The main floor held store goods, while meetings, town gatherings, dances, and plays took place on the second floor. in 1888, the building claimed the fame of becoming the first home of Snow College.

When the ZCMI store closed and the college moved to the Noyes Building on its current campus a block away, the building was used for businesses as varied as a farm implement store to a car repair garage to Ephraim Roller Mills.

Eventually abandoned on its 100 North Main Street location, the building gradually deteriorated to the point that it faced demolition. Then a grass roots effort restored it to its current status as the Ephraim Co-op, a craft shop that offers homemade wares from local artisans.

One night, the volunteer cashier was putting away the broom she'd used to sweep the floor when her husband arrived to give her a ride home. Flicking off the main lights, he followed her into the closet In the dimness of the security lights to steal a kiss. As they snuggled, the stairwell light suddenly flicked on.

Startled, they pushed the partly closed door open to see who'd come into the building. A lady clothed in a long dress like one from the pioneer era stood just outside the closet. Shaking her finger at the husband and wife, she said, "Now you stop that! It's time for you to leave."

The astonished couple looked at one another to

verify that they were both seeing the same thing. When they turned back to ask the woman how she'd gotten in, she was gone.

Co-op member Eleanor Gaddy explains that at a bottom of a staircase leading the second floor, a wooden gate makes a distinctive sound whenever it's moved. Nearly every day at 5:30 pm, the gate makes that sound, even if is no one's in the store but the cashier. The movement is not caused by drafts of air from the heater or air conditioner, either, because it happens even if they are turned off.

"I know when it's 5:30 because that gate goes," Eleanor says with a smile. "It's not every day, but it's often enough that I notice it. This ghost keeps a time schedule."

One of the craft store volunteers told Eleanor that even on a windless day, it is not unusual for the front door to push open of its own accord. Besides that, the back door apparently locks itself. "We have people come in, and some other people come right after them, and the door's locked," Eleanor says. "There's no reason the door would lock. We've tried and tried to do it ourselves by opening and closing the door, but it never works. It has to be the ghost."

None of these odd events raise the hairs on Eleanor's neck, but a visitor who claimed to be a "sensitive," meaning that she can sense spirits, had a hair-raising experience. After walking into the store, the customer suddenly stopped and asked Eleanor, "Has anything weird taken place in this building?"

"There have been a few things," Eleanor said. "Why do you ask?"

The customer beckoned to Eleanor. "Walk with me." Eleanor followed the woman toward the stairs. As soon as they reached the self-moving gate,

Eleanor was startled to see the other woman's short hair stand up on end.

"There is definitely someone here," the customer said, her gaze thoughtful. "Her name is Martha. She was a cook."

Recalling that the co-op building's walls were once part of Fort Ephraim, Eleanor wondered if Martha had been a cook at the fort back in the 1800's. Whoever she is, Eleanor declares, "Martha is a very friendly entity. She's not malevolent. We've never had any bad feelings about her at all."

Is the force behind the front door opening of its own accord a cook named Martha from the fort's pioneer days? Does the gate move from the unseen hand of someone heading upstairs for a routine 5:30 meeting? Could the locked back door be a former business owner keeping the old place secure? Or did the amorous couple see a former Snow College student or teacher who is still watching over the place that was once used for higher learning?

Locked Safe

Kathy Rowe grew up in a mortuary. It was a perfectly normal childhood, since her parents owned Ursenbach Funeral Home in Mt. Pleasant, Utah. Walking among caskets laid out in the display room was as ordinary for Kathy as a walk through a garden. Her family home was right next door, allowing Kathy to spend as much time around funeral preparations as she did in her own living room. Perhaps her prolonged exposure to the recently deceased sharpened her sense of spiritual awareness, but her mother also got feelings about spirits around her, so it could have been a family trait. Wherever it came from, it was accepted as a regular way of life.

After Kathy married Alan, he laughed at her insistence that she sometimes felt spirits at the funeral home, claiming it was her over-active imagination from childhood.

When Kathy's father passed away, her mother wanted to put his VFW (Veterans of Foreign Wars) cap on display at his viewing. As a member of the VFW group, Dad was entitled to wear the specialized cap, reserved for members only, while hosting official events. Mom asked Alan to get the cap from the funeral coach (hearse.)

Not finding it in the coach, Alan wen to look for it in the office. Putting his hand on the doorknob, he began to turn it when he stopped, suddenly struck with the conviction that he shouldn't go in. Although it was supposed to be empty, he felt sure that someone was in there. He knew who it was, too. If he went in the office, he'd be intruding on his father and grandfather-in-law, the funeral home owner before

Kathy's dad.

Alan returned to Kathy and her mother to tell them he hadn't found the cap, and explain what had happened to him at the office. He admitted to Kathy that his experience at the office door was so strong that he would never doubt her ability to feel spirits again.

A couple of days later, the heirs went into the office to sort out Dad's business papers from the safe. Only three living people knew the combination - Kathy, her brother, and their mother.

Strangely enough, although all three of them tried the combination, the lock refused to budge. Kathy was especially perplexed, since she routinely got into the safe once a week. Although she was sure she remembered correctly, she double checked her hidden prompt just to make sure they were using the right access code.

They were.

At last, the family had to call a locksmith who specialized in safes. What he found was startling.

The safe's combination had been changed.

The only way to change the access code was from inside the open safe, yet none of the three surviving family members had opened the safe since Kathy's father passed away. Suspecting robbery, they studied the contents, but nothing had been disturbed.

How had the combination lock been changed? Was Dad trying to get a message to them that he still had a hand in the business? Had he and his father contrived the combination change to remind their posterity that life was uncertain, and there was more to living than just doing business?

It's Cold Upstairs

When Amy Willden got a job at Utah Heritage Credit Union in Ephraim, she thought it was charming the way the company had refurbished an old home on Main Street into a place of business. But her appreciation of its quaint nature changed to apprehension the summer day she was sent upstairs to one of the former bedrooms to retrieve a file.

The item she was after was stored in the second room along the narrow upstairs hallway. The first room was for keeping seasonal decorations to spruce up the credit union on holidays.

Since the second floor was only used for storage, running air conditioning up there wasn't a priority, so a wave of heat hit Amy as she topped the stairs. No matter. She wouldn't be up there long. She'd just grab the file and go.

Yet as she walked past the room jumbled with decorations, a sudden rush of air shot out through the doorway, so cold it made the flesh on her bare arms tingle. Not only that, Amy felt the sensation of someone walking up behind her so strongly that she turned around. She expected to see someone from the downstairs office with a spray bottle of water, playing a joke on the new girl. But no one was there.

What was going on? Amy made a cautious circuit of the upstairs rooms, checking to see if any windows were open. They were all closed tight. She glanced up at the ceilings to see if there was any explanation for the cold breeze, but no air conditioning had been installed without her knowledge.

Feeling the back of her neck prickle, Amy managed to locate the file with clumsy fingers, grabbed it, and hurried back down the stairs without a backward glance. Was that a whispery laugh she heard echoing in the stairwell behind her?

What had caused the rush of cold air and made Amy feel as if she were being followed? Could it have been the ghost of a former resident, seeking an explanation for the stacks of decorations piled in his or her bedroom?

The Candle

On Christmas Eve 2002, Amy Willden had an experience that she still can't explain. While driving home from a family Christmas party with her husband, Justin, and 3-year-old daughter, Savannah, the city's power went out. After making their way home in the chilly darkness of a frosty night, they locked themselves in and snuggled on the bed, watching the cheery flame of a candle on a nearby table. Still excited from celebrating with cousins at Grandma's house, Savannah had a hard time falling asleep.

Amy's thoughts were also full, mostly of reminiscing with family about her beloved great grandma, who'd died shortly after Christmas the year before.

Savannah finally lay down on a pillow when Justin stroked her hair. It looked like she was about to fall asleep when the candle suddenly flamed up so brightly that Amy stared at it in surprise.

Savannah turned to look at the towering flame, her face brightening. She sat up and called, "Hi!," with a smile and a wave at the impossibly tall flame.

"What's going on?" Justin asked, frowning as the light's reflection danced in his eyes.

"I don't know," Amy replied.

Savannah glanced at her parents with delight, then turned back to the candle and repeated, "Hi!" with a cheerful wave.

"Who are you waving at?" Amy asked.

"The lady." Savannah pointed at the candle, then swept her joyful gaze over her parents.

"What lady?" Justin asked, sitting up straight and squinting into the dimness beyond the eerily bright flame.

At the same time, Amy said, "There's no lady there."

Savannah frowned. "By the fire," she insisted, pointing. Then she smiled and waved again, repeating, "Hi! Hi!"

Amy tried to see what her daughter saw, but to her eyes, there was only an empty room beyond the candle.

When Justin threw his legs over the side of the bed, Savannah's smile relaxed. The little girl dropped her arm, lay back on the pillow with a happy sigh, and closed her eyes. Amy and Justin exchanged a glance just as the candle flame died down to its previous tame flicker.

"That was so odd," Amy whispered.

Justin slid off the bed, declaring, "I'm going to see if a window's open. Maybe a draft of air was blowing across the flame."

As expected on a frosty winter night, all of the windows were shut tight.

What made the candle flare up so high? Had

Great Grandma really come back for a Christmas Eve visit? Did the family reminiscing bring her back? If so, why was Savannah the only one who could see her? Was it because she didn't think it was impossible for Great Grandma to be there?

Ghost on a Horse

Alva Larsen loved his horse almost as much as he loved his family, spending hours riding in the cool solace of the neighboring mountains. As a man in his forties, he expected to spend many more years enjoying his time on horseback, but it was not to be. A sudden heart attack overtook him while he was out walking, ending his life before he reached the age of fifty.

Even though he died, a photograph in the possession of his granddaughter, Cassidie Larsen, may show that he is not completely gone.

After Alva's unexpected passing, his son, Terry, decided to honor his father by taking his horse on a final walk into the mountains as a way to commemorate Alva's life. Riding his own horse, Terry took the lead rope of Alva's horse and started off through the trees while Alva's sister, Colleen, captured the moment with her camera. Her vision blurred by tears, Colleen snapped the picture from where she stood behind the departing horses.

After his final walk through familiar mountain trails, Alva's horse was sold.

In this time before digital cameras, Colleen took her roll of film to be developed. When the prints were ready, Colleen shuffled through the stack of photos.

Suddenly she stopped at the picture of Alva's horse following Terry on his ride toward the wooded mountainside. What was that on Alva's horse? She looked closer, studying the image in bewilderment, not sure she could believe what she saw.

Heart pounding, she decided she had to show the picture to other family members. She wouldn't tell them what she'd seen. She would wait to hear what they had to say first.

Her suspicions were verified by the first person she showed. Eyes widening at the sight of the filmy white image on the saddle of the riderless horse, Terry said exactly what Colleen had been thinking. "It looks like Dad's still riding his horse."

Was the ghostly image a trick of shadow and light, or a defect on the film? If so, why didn't any of the other pictures from the same roll show any shadows like this single photo? Had Alva come back for a final ride on his beloved horse, preferring to leave life in the saddle that on foot? Or could it be that he'd been taken so suddenly that he simply wanted to spend a little more time with his family?

Keeping A Promise

Being in a wheelchair didn't stop Grandpa Kenneth Christensen from driving his two grandchildren to school. Nine-year-old Selena hopped out of the car before her ten-year-old sister, Alisa, calling, "Thanks, Grandpa."

Grandpa winked at her. "You can ride in my magic chariot any time. "

Alisa smiled and echoed, "Thanks."

"Hey, girls, summer's just around the corner. How about if we plan our summer vacation when you get home today?"

"But we still have three weeks of school," Alisa said.

Grandpa gave the steering wheel a cheerful slap. "Like I said, right around the corner!"

"Can we go to the zoo?" Selena asked.

"I want to go to Disneyland," Alisa said.

"We'll talk about every place you want to go," Grandpa promised. Then he held up hand. "And if I happen to stop and get some ice cream after school, I'll need someone to help me eat it."

"I will!" Alisa offered eagerly.

"Me, too," Selena added.

"It's a date," Grandpa said, smiling. "I'll come pick you up after school." He drove away while his granddaughters headed for class, talking eagerly about their upcoming summer adventures with Grandpa.

Before morning recess, a Salt Lake County police officer came to Selena's classroom. Startled by his presence, Selena was alarmed to see Alisa standing with him, looking small and confused. The officer said something in a low voice to Selena's teacher, who then turned toward her. "You need to go with this policeman, Selena."

Squirming under the gazes of all her classmates, Selena asked, "Why?"

"It's all right," her teacher said solemnly. "He'll tell you outside."

Selena caught up to her sister and they clasped hands, following the tall policeman out into the hall. Instead of telling the girls why he was there, the officer said, "We'll let your mother explain things when you get home."

"Is Mom okay?" Alisa asked, her voice full of uncertainty.

"She's fine," the officer assured her, leading the way out to the police car and letting the girls in. "Please buckle your seat belts."

As he started the car, Selena asked, "Why won't you tell us what's wrong?"

Alisa leaned forward, her seatbelt folding her in half at her waist. "Is it something bad?"

The officer sighed. "Your mother will tell you all about it."

Mom opened the door before they even reached it, looking strange with her red, puffy eyes. After thanking the officer, she led her girls toward the living room.

"Why did he get us from school?" Selena asked.

"It wasn't even over yet," Alisa added.

"Let's sit down," Mom said. After pressing a tissue to her mouth, Mom pulled it away, took a deep breath, and said, "Grandpa was on his way to get some breakfast after he dropped you girls off when a drunk driver ran into him." Mom's eyes brimmed with fresh tears, and her voice broke. "Grandpa died. I'm so sorry."

Selena shook her head as a sudden wave of relief coursed through her. "Mom, he's not dead."

After a moment of shocked silence, her mother offered a shaky smile. "I know it seems like he's still here when he took you to school just this morning," she said gently. "It happened so suddenly, it's hard to believe."

"No, Mom. You're wrong," Selena insisted. She pointed at Grandpa's chair. "He's sitting right there looking at us with a big smile on his face." Selena lowered her hand and looked at her mother. "If he's sitting right there, he can't be dead, can he?"

Selena's mother turned to stare at Grandpa's chair. Then she faced Selena. "Don't do this, honey," she said. "We just have to accept it."

Selena glanced back at Grandpa's chair, puzzled to see that it was suddenly empty. She tried explaining again to her mother that she'd just seen him, but couldn't make her mother believe that Grandpa had been sitting there when the girls walked in.

Later that night, Selena sat alone in the living room, staring at the floor, thinking of Grandpa. When she looked up, there he was sitting in his chair again. "Grandpa!" she cried. "Mom thinks you're dead. You need to tell her you aren't."

"Oh, Selena, honey," Grandpa said. "You're mom's right. I am dead. I just came back for a few minutes because I don't want any of you to worry about me. Look at this!" He stood, spreading his hands to show that he didn't need a wheelchair. Jumping up, he clicked his heels together. "What do you think of that?"

Selena stared at him, hardly recognizing her grandpa as he stood on two feet.

"Nothing hurts," Grandpa said with his warm, familiar smile. "And do you know what else? My mom and dad are over here, too!" Grandpa's face grew serious. "I want you to be happy for me, honey, because I'm happy. Did you know that life is kind of like school? So how about when you're all done with the school of life, I come back and pick you up?"

Selena nodded, her heart full of love as she watched her beloved Grandpa's smiling face fade away.

A few years later, Selena was in the kitchen fixing lunch with her six-year-old brother, Lee, who was born after Grandpa died. Suddenly, Lee asked, "Who's that man?"

Surprised, Selena looked up. Seeing no one else in the kitchen, she replied, "I don't know what you're talking about."

Later that night, when Selena told Mom what Lee had said, Mom pulled out some old pictures. As soon as Lee saw a photo of Grandpa, he jumped up and said, "Selena, that's the man I saw in the kitchen with you!"

Was Ken traveling back and forth between worlds to look out for his family? Was he interested in getting to know the grandson he'd never met? Did he appear to Selena when she was younger in order to keep his promise to see her after school, whether he was dead or alive?

Things That Move in the Night

One Sunday, Noah Cano's family went to church, leaving fifteen-year-old Noah home alone. Everything was quiet, until Noah heard a strange noise coming from the bathroom. It sounded like a big bird flapping its wings. How could a bird have gotten into the house?

Heart pounding, Noah got up and sidled to the bathroom. Easing open the door, he caught sight of the shower curtain billowing in and out, in and out, as if the tub were breathing.

Swallowing past sudden dryness in his throat, Noah called, "Who's there?"

No one answered, but the shower curtain abruptly fell still. The following silence was just as eerie as the strange noise.

His neck prickling with fear, Noah slammed the door and hurried to his room, shutting himself in.

Then he heard it again, the steady *flap, flap,* of the shower curtain swaying in and out. He wouldn't going back there. Instead, he turned on some music and tried to ignore the weirdness in the bathroom as he waited for his family to return.

By the time their car pulled up to the house, the shower curtain hung still. Noah hurried to greet them, counting everyone as they gathered in the kitchen for dinner, verifying that no one else had stayed home but him. Everyone was present and accounted for, except for Noah's sister who would have been three years older than him if she hadn't tragically died in a car accident when she was two. Of course she wasn't there, was she?

When Noah told his family about the mysterious moving shower curtain, his father said he must have had the air conditioner on, making an air current that stirred up the curtain. Noah insisted that he hadn't. His mother said there must be a window open. Noah immediately made a circuit of the house, but found no open windows.

From that time on, it seemed that when Noah was home alone, the shower curtain frequently flapped with no wind. It stopped when he went in to check, and started again after he left the room.

If this wasn't weird enough, one day when his friend Jason Jurado was staying overnight, they were startled awake at 1:00 am when the spring-style door stopper vibrated with a noisy *sproing!* Jason's head shot up from his pillow. Squinting through the darkness at Noah, he asked, "What was that?"

"I don't know."

Sproing!

The boys got up and cautiously walked across the room, staring at the spring doorstop sticking out from the bottom of the door. There was no one there to make the door stop vibrate.

"Who flicked it?" Josh asked.

"I don't know."

As the two friends turned away to return to bed, they heard the sound of quick, light footsteps. Then came the distinct sound of the door stop vibrating. *Sproing!*

Jason shivered. "This is really creepy."

"I'm not staying up here." Noah grabbed a blanket and pillow. Jason did, too. They scurried downstairs, intending to sleep on the couch until morning.

They each plopped a pillow on either end of the couch, their feet squirming for space on the cushions between them. Once they were settled in, Noah felt as if he might finally get some rest.

He was just drifting off to sleep when the TV turned on.

Jason sat up, his face appearing greenish in the reflected light from the screen. Hair sticking up like a fright wig, he pulled the blanket up under his chin. "Why'd you turn that on?"

Noah's wide eyes took in the image of a cat dancing across the screen while its owner shook a box of cat food over its head. "I didn't."

"Then who did?"

"I don't know."

The boys stared at the freakish cat while the sound of footsteps moved toward them down the hallway, growing louder with each step. Remembering the footsteps upstairs, Noah stared at the doorway with mounting dread. When his mother appeared, Noah nearly screamed with relief.

"What are you boys doing?" she whispered, closing in on the television and turning it off, leaving the room darkly silent.

"We didn't do it," Noah protested as his mother flicked on a lamp.

Jason squinted against the light. "Honest, it turned on by itself. We were sleeping."

"Now, boys, why are you down here instead of upstairs?"

"We got scared," Noah admitted. "Mom, I think we have a ghost. Sometimes the dog barks at nothing I can see. Animals can sense ghosts, you know."

Mrs. Cano sat down on the chair across from the boys, sighed, and ran her hand through her dark hair.

"Really, Mom, the other day I heard someone walking in the hall and when I looked, there was no one there. There wasn't time for anyone to hide. And it just happened again upstairs."

"And someone was playing with the door stopper," Jason added.

"Nothing here will hurt you," Mrs. Cano said.

"Do you know what it is?" Noah watched his mother closely, hoping for some reasonable answer.

"Not exactly."

"But what do you think?"

"It's just that sometimes I hear a baby crying upstairs," Mrs. Cano admitted softly.

"Whose baby?" Jason asked.

Mrs. Cano spread her hands. "That's just it. There

is no baby here anymore." She paused, then glanced at the doorway. "But it sounds like my little girl who died."

"Do you think...she's...here? Now?" Noah asked.

Mrs. Cano rubbed a hand across her eyes. "I don't know. But if she is, how could she hurt you? She's only two." Noah's mother got a far-off look in her eyes.

"But maybe she grew up in ghost years," Jason blurted. "Maybe she's an older ghost now."

Mrs. Cano gave Jason a sad-eyed look. "It doesn't matter. I'm probably just imagining it." She stood and gazed at the photo of her holding her baby daughter taken just a few weeks before the accident.

"Do you really think it's her?" Noah whispered, but his mother didn't seem to hear him. She flicked off the lamp, then walked off into the darkness, whispering something that sounded like, "Now let your brother sleep."

Is Noah's dog barking at his sister? Is she playing the games she used to play when she was alive with the shower curtain and the doorstop? Is she trying to get her little brother Noah to play with her?

Night Walking

Teenager Jaden Robinson is reluctant to share her queen-sized bed with her ten-year-old sister, Kylie. It's not that she doesn't like her sister, it's because Kylie sometimes exhibits bizarre behavior after the lights are out. "She'll sit up in the middle of the night," Jaden says. "Her eyes are open and it looks like she's staring into your soul while she talks." Jaden shivers. "Her words don't make any sense, and sometimes she screams at you. She's not really awake, but she looks like she is."

While Kylie has been waking up in the night since she was a baby, her late night walks in the dark didn't start until three years ago.

Jaden was on her phone in the front room at 11:30 p.m. when she saw eight-year-old Kylie walk out of their bedroom. "What are you doing?" Jaden asked.

Wordlessly, Kylie turned to stare at Jaden.

"You're creeping me out," Jaden complained.

Without a word, Kylie walked out of the room, but Jaden didn't dare follow her. Twenty minutes later, Kylie returned and fell into a sound sleep.

On another night, Jaden watched Kylie walk into the kitchen, open the knife drawer, take the knives out, and wander through the house, placing knives in various locations. Again, she didn't dare stop her sister's actions, not knowing if she'd snap.

The next morning, Jaden asked why she'd done it. Kylie's eyes went wide. "I didn't."

"Yes, you did," Jaden insisted. "I saw you."

Kylie refused to believe her, but Jaden's friend, Steph, is a witness to Kylie's strange night walking. "Once when we were watching a movie, she came out of her room and stood so close to the fire in the fireplace that I thought she might get hurt. Before I could say anything, she started throwing things at Jaden and me, screaming, 'You're so fat and ugly.' It was kind of funny, but scary, too."

Woken by the yelling, Kylie's mother came out of her room and took her younger daughter back to bed. The next morning, Kylie didn't remember a single thing about the incident.

In spite of the fact that she's been startled by occasionally waking up on the kitchen floor, Jaden reports that Kylie insists, "I don't have a problem."

Jaden disagrees, declaring that Jaden was so scared on the night that Kylie woke up and pointed to something in the room that she refused to look. It wasn't the first time Kylie had done this, but with a weird feeling that something was actually there, Jaden hid her head under her pillow instead.

These days when Kylie first wakes up in the dark, Jaden gives her a shove and says, "Go back to sleep."

And Kylie does.

What causes Kylie's strange night time behavior? Is it ordinary sleepwalking that a few other people experience? Or is there really someone - or something - in her room calling to her, urging her toward her strange nocturnal ways?

The Night They Died

One morning, fifteen-year-old Katelyn Dickinson woke up sobbing. It was 4:00 am. As she wiped her tears, chest heaving in tortured gasps, she was amazed to realize that she must have been crying in her sleep.

Unable to stop crying, she sat up and discovered that things were even weirder. Her feet were on her pillow and her head was at the foot of her bed.

Frightened, Katelyn stumbled to her mother's room and stood in the doorway, nearly hysterical as she tried to speak through her tears.

Her mother sat up and asked, "Katelyn, what's wrong?"

"I… don't know," Katelyn managed to stammer.

Her mother got out of bed, put an arm around her, and led her downstairs. When they were seated in the living room, her mother said, "Tell me what you can."

Safe in the circle of her mother's arms, Katelyn recalled the vague memory of someone asking her what was so important about the 18th. Katelyn had answered, "That's the day Luke and Steven died."

Katelyn's friend, fourteen-year-old Luke, and his seven-year-old brother, Steven, were snowmobiling in the mountains near Heber, Utah, when they were caught in a deadly avalanche. Neither one survived.

For the first few months after the accident, Katelyn was starkly aware of the morbid reminder whenever the 18th day of each month arrived, unconsciously tracking the time since she'd lost her friends. After several months passed, life events seemed to dull the sharp reminder of the 18th, and it began slipping past her without particular note.

As Katelyn explained to her mother what she could remember about events before she woke up crying, they both realized that it was the 18th.

It was a year since Katelyn's friends had died.

Why did Katelyn wake up crying on the tragic anniversary when she hadn't consciously registered the date for the past couple of months? Had her subconscious mind chronicled the date and stirred up a dream about her terrible loss on that day? Or had her friends come for a nocturnal visit on the anniversary of their passing?

Still Shopping

In honor of her small town convenience store that's been in business for decades, Cathee decorates the walls with historical photos of the town. In 2015, one of those old time black and white photos of a building in the center of town flew off the wall and clattered to the floor. There was no explanation. No one had opened or shut a door, there was no wind, and none of the surrounding pictures, fastened to the wall in the same way, had moved an inch.

That's not the only strange occurrence in the old store. On other days, licorice rope boxes have launched off the shelf with enough force to fly across the room.

A possible clue to the invisible culprit appeared when an employee mopped the floor after hours. Suddenly he stopped swiping the mop back and forth to stare at the expanse of floor he'd just cleaned. "Cathee," he called, "come take a look at this!"

When Cathee approached the shining floor, her eyes widened in surprise at the child-sized footprints tracking across the wetness. There were no children in the closed store.

One of Cathee's employees named Sandi actually saw the child who could be the source of the footprints. It was a day when Sandi helped close the store early, much to the disappointment of four children standing on the sidewalk, looking longingly in through the locked glass front door.

Suddenly, Sandi stopped sweeping, startled to see a boy walking across the floor toward the soda pop display. How had he gotten in? Sandi watched the boy walk up to the register where Cathee concentrated on balancing the till, fully expecting Cathee to tell the boy he'd have to leave because they were closed. When Cathee didn't say a word or even glance at the child, Sandi wondered if he was someone Cathee knew or was related to, so she'd let him in. He was a stranger to Sandi, wearing scruffy old fashioned overalls and a plaid shirt. Could he be a foster child?

Sandi finally asked, "Do you want me to tell him we're closed?"

Cathee's head came up, her brow creased in puzzlement. "Who?"

Now it was Sandi's turn to looked confused. "That boy." She pointed at him.

Cathee scanned the room, eyebrows raised. "There's no one here but you and me."

Multiple knocks on the door made Sandi jump and turn to see the children pressing their noses against the door, both hands cupped around their faces. One of them tried the handle, but it didn't give.

"We're closed," Sandi called, wondering if she'd left the back door by the kitchen unlocked, allowing the boy in overalls a way in.

"Then why is he in there?" a muffled voice called through the glass while a grubby finger pointed at the boy wandering past the penny candy display.

The other children nodded, gazing with envy at the privileged child.

"Who are you talking about?" Cathee asked, coming out from behind the register.

"The kid behind you," the children called, pointing even more emphatically.

Cathee turned, but only saw Sandi in the room. She told the children, "There's no one here but the two of us."

"Is too."

"Uh, uh."

"He's right there!"

Sandi glanced toward the boy, trying to understand why Cathee couldn't see him. To her surprise, the boy was gone.

On another day after closing, Sandi heard the distinct sound of someone humming an old fashioned tune after the doors were locked. Searching the store to see who'd stayed behind after hours, she was surprised to find that she was the only one in the building.

Sandi's not the only one who's detected a presence in the store. Some employees report a glimpse of what looks like a person, then it's suddenly gone. "A couple of weeks ago, another coworker was behind the bar and I was in front," Sandi explains. That's when they both heard someone walking in the storage room and through the kitchen. Then they were startled to hear the sudden exclamation, "Hey!' When Sandi went looking for the unauthorized visitor, there was no one there.

The next morning when Cathee opened the store, she found not only the salt and pepper shakers tipped over and spilled, but the chairs sitting on the floor. When she asked Sandi about it, Sandi insisted that they'd put the chairs up on the table for mopping, and the shakers were all upright when they left and locked the door.

It seems that some entity might hold a grudge, or else thinks it's funny to throw things. Sandi watched a kitchen spatula inexplicably fly toward Cathee before it arced downward and landed on the ground.

Another time after Cathee's daughter, Nikki, helped Sandi close the store, they were halfway home when Cathee called to report that the store security alarm was going off. The two women hurried back to the store. The alarm was silent. When they unlocked the door and went inside, the alarm blared. In spite of the noise, Nikki and Sandi heard someone moving around downstairs. Since Sandi and Nikki have both seen a man walking from the doorway into the refrigerator and disappear, they weren't surprised when the police showed up and found no one else in the store.

Sometimes the back kitchen door opens by itself. One night Sandi thought someone had come in, because she heard the back door open and footsteps move into the kitchen. When she looked to see who it was, she didn't see anyone. "I had goosebumps from head to toe," Sandi says. "It was crazy. I knew there was someone there, but I just didn't know who." Sandi's also heard somebody walking on the steps from downstairs to the top, yet there's no one there.

Sandi believes there are at least three ghosts haunting the store. Besides the man who disappears into the refrigerator, there's the little boy she's seen, and a lady's voice she heard say, "Dave." That's the reason the staff tends to say, "Oh, Dave, knock it off," whenever something unexplained happens.

Sandi is not afraid of the ghostly activity. On the contrary, she says, "It's pretty neat. I like things like this. Sometimes it's really active. I'd like someone to come in here and do a reading or something."

Why do mysterious things happen in the old country store? Are they caused by the ordinary sounds from settling of an old building? Or are there former employees still working the store, and small patrons still hoping for a piece of candy?

Ignored

When Ruth Anderson and her husband bought a modest house in Manti, Utah, at a price that included all its contents, they didn't realize that those contents included a ghost.

The older couple who lived in the house drifted apart after their children left home. The husband routinely got up early, fixed his own breakfast, and left the house for most of the day while his wife stayed home, spending most of the day sitting in her upholstered living room chair.

On a day when one of their daughters came to visit, she was horrified to find her mother slumped in her chair, dead. She called the authorities, who reported that the woman had been dead for at least two days.

Her husband hadn't even noticed. He'd gone on with his usual routine, preparing his meals, washing his dishes, and walking past his wife's chair as he came and went without a word or a glance in her direction.

A couple of years after his wife was buried, the widower died, leaving a house full of old things that his children were reluctant to sort through. After taking a few personal effects, they let their childhood home go.

Once the house was emptied of decades of clutter, and freshened up with paint and new carpet, renters eagerly moved in. Five months later, they moved out.

Next on the renter list was a young couple who happily set up house in the cozy cottage. Six months later, they told the Anderson's they were leaving. This time, the landlords got an explanation. "The house is haunted, and the ghost is not very nice."

When Ruth related the unusual complaint to some of her friends, she learned of a woman named Jansen who claimed the ability to talk to spirits. Ruth contacted her, and Jansen agreed to help.

Bringing three of her friends to the house, Ruth followed Jansen's instructions to have everyone stand in a circle. Then Jansen closed her eyes and called, "We know you are here. We would just like to talk to you. Please come to us."

Before long, Jansen began speaking as if she were carrying on a conversation, but no one else could hear anyone answering her. They listened to her explain that a woman's spirit was staying in the house. The spirit was so angry about being ignored for so long after she died that she didn't want to go anywhere.

Jansen told the spirit that it would be much better for her if she would go to the light. She explained there were kind beings there who would not ignore her. They loved her and wanted her to be with them.

Eventually, Jansen stopped reasoning with the spirit and turned to the others in the room. She reported that the spirit had followed her advice, and was now gone.

From then on, the renters stayed.

Did the old woman's ghost remain in the house after her death in order to keep her husband company? Or was it to berate him for not even noticing she was dead? Once he died, was she so used to living in the same house that she didn't know where else to go? Or did she simply resist going to the place where he might still be coming and going without even looking at her?

Musical Ghost

Captivated by the quaint oolite stone and brick Victorian pioneer house she found in Gunnison, Utah, Claudia Sanborn bought it, not knowing it came with a ghost.

While looking into her home's history, Claudia discovered that it had been home to Anthony Metcalf, a miller who served as city councilman and constable, as well as two terms as Gunnison's mayor. Impressed, Claudia took the necessary steps to get the home listed on Utah's Historic Register.

Interestingly enough, as Claudia delved further into the family's history, she discovered that Anthony's wife, Sylvia, not only had fifteen children, but she sewed the sacks for the flour from her husband's mill. If that weren't enough, she also served as a practical nurse and midwife. Since Claudia is a nurse, this bit of information gave her the comforting sense that her ownership of the house was meant to be.

After decades of welcoming visitors into her home, which became known as the halfway house for weary travelers, Nurse Metcalf died at the age of 101. In her day, viewings were held in the house. It doesn't bother Claudia that the former owner was laid out in her living room after she passed away, because Claudia says, "There wasn't anything tragic that happened here in this house that I know of."

One thing Claudia can't help wondering is if one of the original owners was a music lover, because she can't explain how music plays unexpectedly through her house at random moments. "Every once in awhile, we hear the radio playing when no one turned it on,"

Claudia says.

Although Claudia doesn't know the identity of the musical ghost, she says her brush with the unexplained is amiable, because the Metcalf's were a friendly family. In spite of the mysterious music, Claudia still feels like her home is a safe haven.

What makes the radio play music when no one physically turns it on? Is there a short in the old electrical wiring? Could it be that one of the Metcalf children is exploring technology that wasn't available in their day? Or does Sylvia Metcalf herself appreciate a little music while she walks the rooms of her former home?

White Wolf

Cameron is haunted by images of something that his friend, an ecclesiastical missionary named Hughes, experienced while on a religious mission in Arizona.

"He was riding shotgun in a car as his missionary companion was driving," Cameron explains. "While moving along the highway, he was startled to see a white wolf beside the road." Excited, Hughes pointed out the animal to his companion, but his amazement turned to terror when he watched the wolf stand up on its hind legs as easily as a man.

Then things got worse. Impossibly, the wolf ran alongside the car, keeping pace at highway speed.

"He was being hunted in his own car by a skin walker," Cameron reports.

A skin walker appears in some Native American

legends as a malevolent being. Not a demon, werewolf, or creature, it's reportedly an actual person (usually naked) wearing animal hide and a necklace with a single turquoise bead. They also tend to paint their faces white, and possess witch-like skills.

A skin walker is also identified as a shaman, or medicine man. Childless females may also be witches or skin walkers, although they are less common than men. While not every witch is a skin walker, every skin walker is considered a witch. Some legends propose that the transformation from human to animal can only be accomplished if the skin walker wears the animal's pelt.

To ward off these frightening beings, most Native American tribes have a tradition against whistling at night, because it's thought to attract skin walkers. They're not known for murdering people to steal their skins and assume their identity, but no one wants them near. Perhaps it's because of the frightening belief is that they must kill a close relative in order to become a skin walker in the first place.

To create harm, they use an "evil way" ceremony, which is meant to cause the victim misery, ranging from bad luck to illness to a painful, prolonged death. In some Native American cultures, a skin walker uses dead people's powdered bones to paralyze another victim.

Their main ability is said to be turning into any animal he or she desires. They are also said to be able to jump incredibly high, be invulnerable to damage (again, a relative is usually used to unwittingly take the brunt of the injury), and run incredibly fast, as fast as a car on a highway.

Did Hughes actually see a white wolf skin walker running beside his car? Could it have been a trick of light and shadow? If it was real, then why was a skin walker targeting missionaries? Was it bent on destruction? Or did it want to hear their message?

Native American Spirit

When Sue Player examined the old Utah house she bought, she found a substance on the floor that she describes as looking suspiciously like blood. Exploring further, she discovered a place in the basement where it appeared that the blood-like substance had dripped down the walls from the edges of the floor above. "I'm pretty sure someone died in there," Sue says. "It may have been from a farming accident between 1885 and 1902."

Subsequent events caused Sue to change her mind.

After moving in, Sue made sure the floors and walls were cleaned up, but that didn't end the strangeness. Not only did some of her things mysteriously go missing, but she a strong feeling overcame her. Whatever was happening in her house was from something older than the era of white men coming to the west. She doesn't believe that all the ghosts she's encountered are immigrants.

Her feelings of having a Native American spirit nearby intensified when she took her Yorkie/Schnauzer mix dog, Haley, on a petroglyph exploration one hot summer day. The dog and owner traveled with a couple of friends to a place south of Fillmore, Utah, where lots of ancient artwork is marked on volcanic rock.

As soon as Sue opened the car door, a wall of 114 degree Fahrenheit air slammed into her. Anxious to run free, Haley jumped out of the car. As soon as her paws touched the scorching hot sand, she let out a scream like a tortured human.

Frightened, Sue snatched up her dog, certain that Haley's feet had burned. To her surprise, Haley stopped crying. When Sue examined her feet, they looked perfectly normal.

With Haley firmly in her arms, Sue and her friends looked at the rock art before piling back into the air-conditioned car to return home.

The next day, Sue noticed something strange on Haley's back. In one spot, the fur was changing color. Three days later, the color was deeper, showing a more pronounced shape. In a week's time, the distinct outline of a walking man, in the style of a petroglyph, was clearly visible in the dog's fur.

Sue took several pictures of the unexplained image as it developed over the course of several days. The image remained for about a month before it slowly faded away.

When Sue met a Native American woman, she told her of the strange occurrence. Sue tried to bring up the digital pictures of the image, but to her surprise, they were gone. The photos taken before and after Haley's transformation were still there, but there were no pictures of the image in Haley's fur. They had all inexplicably disappeared from her camera.

The Native American was not surprised. She explained that when Haley's feet were burned, she was touched by the spirits in that place and instantly healed.

Is it possible that burns on Haley's feet were healed by Native American spirits who didn't want an innocent animal to suffer? Or was her pain caused by jarring her leg?

What created the image on her fur? Was it some type of bizarre canine sunburn? Or was it impressed on the dog by invisible spirits touching her with spiritual hands while easing her distress?

Coming and Going

Lauri Rosier Clark never mentioned the spirits she saw bringing brand-new babies to their mothers in the delivery room, because she thought everyone could see them. She also believed that the other hospital employees saw the spirits that came to escort dying patient's spirits away, so she was surprised to learn that it wasn't so. The spirits that came and went, appearing as flesh and blood people of all different ages and clothing styles, were invisible to everyone else at the hospital where she worked.

One day when Lauri was in the emergency room with a dying woman, she watched a man in a suit and a woman dressed in Sunday clothes walk in, holding the hands of an excited little girl in a pink dress. As Lauri watched the girl bounce up and down with joy, she realized that this girl had died as a child. The dying woman was her mother, and the girl could hardly wait to be with her again.

While Lauri has seen the spirits who come to circle the dying body as the machines are turned off abad the body covered, she's never actually witnessed the private event of a spirit leaving its body. A spirit changing from mortal to immortal is not something mortals can comprehend.

Sometimes the spirits who came to usher the dying from mortal life visited Lauri in her lab before fulfilling their assignment. She reports that spirits have distinct personalities just as people in mortality do. She wonders if she had spirit visitors who enjoyed being with a mortal who knew they were there. Sometimes she'd go looking for their loved one. They'd follow her around for a while before she figured out who they were there for. When she walked into the room of the one who was dying, the escort spirits stayed there.

One time, Lauri saw a mother, father, and brother come to get a dying man. Interestingly enough, Lauri noticed that the spirit brother was a bit angry about being there. He liked having his parents to himself in the spirit world, and didn't want to share them with his brother again.

Sibling rivalry aside, while it's usually family who comes to get a loved one, Lauri once observed a spirit figure dressed like a an official church leader collecting a dying person. Lauri could tell that the person on the death bed was not pleased to see the being in the suit waiting for him.

While Lauri saw spirits coming for others, she missed seeing who came to escort her parents to the next life. Her father passed away suddenly on a cold morning after getting out of bed to turn up the heat and get an extra blanket. Once he tossed the blanket over the bed, he lay back down and made an odd gasping sound. When his wife turned toward her husband of 70 years to see what was wrong, he was already gone.

Lauri waited with her father's body for four hours, watching for his spiritual escorts. As the youngest of eleven children, Lauri hoped it would be at least one, or all three, of her brothers who had died in childhood. She wanted to meet them.

She didn't see anyone, but sensed the calming presence of a grandfather she'd never met, her father's brother, and his mother.

When Lauri's mother passed away, Lauri had a similar experience of not seeing the spirits, but knowing that her mother was leaving with loving family members.

In contrast to the peaceful passings she's seen, Lauri has witnessed the horrible sight of dying people who didn't understand where they were going. In at least one instance, when the spirit resisted moving on with all his might, claiming he'd rather do anything than go to the other side, his escort became quite abrasive, giving brusque commands such as, "Come now."

In order to balance out the spirits leaving, guides also bring new spirits into mortality. Female spirits, accompanied by male guardians, always bring the babies into this life. The guardian stands back a respectful distance while the spirit transfer is accomplished. Just as she has not witnessed a spirit leaving a body, Lauri has not been permitted to actually see the spirit transfer into mortal life itself, she just sees the messengers.

In the case of a difficult labor, or if the baby is in trouble, the spirits stay longer, coming and going while the baby's in the hospital, continually checking on him or her.

When Lauri's son was born, he was in the ICU (Intensive Care Unit) from the time he was twenty minutes old until he was two weeks old. The doctors told her that because of his complications, his growth would be stunted and he'd have a harder time in school.

While she didn't see her two deceased grandmothers, Lauri was certain they were in the ICU because the nurses reported that Lauri's baby cried when she left, yet in a few moments he'd abruptly settle down as if someone were giving him a comforting touch.

Even when Lauri took him home, her baby boy wasn't well. With his compromised lungs, breathing was an option, meaning he might breathe, or he might not.

Lauri knew that both her grandmothers had followed her son home to help care for him. Fatigued by the demands of his constant care, Lauri would fall asleep without being aware of it. She'd suddenly awaken from exhausted slumber when her baby was in crisis. She is certain that one of her grandmothers woke her up when the baby needed her.

At eighteen months old, when her son was finally out of imminent danger, Lauri sensed her helpers leave. When her son was two, Lauri held him on her lap while paging through a family photo album. He suddenly pointed at a photograph, exclaiming in delight, "Grandma Rosier." Surprised, Lauri turned the page where he pointed at another picture and declared with a smile, "Grandma Hatch." No one had ever identified the women for him. The only explanation Lauri can come up with is that he recognized them from when they watched over him as a baby.

Lauri credits the care of her ghostly grandmothers for her 6' 4" son's current robust health and accelerated learning programs in school. "His life has always been accelerated," Lauri says. "He's as healthy as can be."

When Lauri's daughter was born, she sensed spirits in attendance, yet without her brother's medical problems, the spirits were not as directly involved in her young life.

Why has Lauri seen those who bring and take spirits from this world, while others haven't? Is it because there are different spiritual gifts, and Lauri has been given a gift for seeing beings that are invisible to most mortals?

Invited

As a divorced mother with a thirteen-year-old daughter, Sheila Summerhays decided to rent out rooms in her Cedar City, Utah basement. Since her daughter, Mindy's, room was in the basement, Sheila thought that taking in a couple of college girls would give Mindy some good role models, as well as supplement the family income. She didn't know those girls would invite unwanted guests.

Sheila and her renters didn't get along, so the arrangement didn't last long. When Sheila found out that the girls were using a Ouija board in her house, she told them to leave.

"What's the big deal?" one of them said, "it's just a piece of wood."

"But what's it for?" Sheila asked.

The girl shrugged. "Playing a game."

"The 'game' is inviting evil to come to you," Sheila scolded.

"We always ask the spirits if they're good or bad," the co-ed said in her own defense.

"They're not going to tell you the truth," Sheila insisted. "You've got to move out now."

Once the girls were gone, Sheila thought the problem was solved. She was surprised to see Mindy sprinting up the stairs one night, eyes bright with terror. "Mom, I can't stand it down there," Mindy said, squeezing her hands in a tight knot.

"Listen, honey, the girls are gone, the board is gone. Just say a prayer before you go to sleep and you'll be fine."

Mindy didn't agree. After a few more days, she announced that she was going to live with her father. Sheila couldn't talk her out of it, so she drove her daughter to the airport and hugged her goodbye.

When she got back home, Sheila carried a load of laundry downstairs to the laundry room. As soon as her foot stepped off the bottom step and touched the basement floor, she felt a presence so evil that she dropped her laundry and ran back up the stairs, screaming.

Mindy was right. The renters had invited the devil into the house.

Sheila rounded up some friends to come over to bless the house. "That took care of it," Sheila says. She never felt another evil thing in her home.

Mindy was back before the semester was over.

Why hadn't Sheila felt any evil in the basement while her daughter was there? Had it targeted Mindy, only turning to Sheila when Mindy was gone?

A Curious Spirit and Vengeful Ghost

When sixteen-year-old Nathan Hoopiiaina was young, he lived in a house with a washing machine ghost. For some reason, an unseen entity was fascinated by the washing machine. While Nathan never saw the ghostly form, he saw what happened when no one was near the washer. "He'd close the washing machine lid and let it spin for a minute, then he'd open it," Nathan explains, "You could see the lid go up and down. It seems like he wanted to watch it spin to see how it worked." Sometimes it happened several times during the spin cycle, and other times the lid only went up and down once.

Nathan suspects that the ghost could be from a time when there were no automatic washing machines. Yet if that's the case, isn't it just as likely that the ghost is a "she" instead of a "he?" After all, what hard-working housewife working her knuckles raw wouldn't trade in her scrub board for an automatic washing machine?

That's not the only ghost Nathan has encountered, but the next one was visible, and wore a trench coat.

"At night I'd hear him walking up and down the hallway outside my bedroom," Nathan says, "or else he'd pace back and forth in the attic."

Once Nathan managed to fall asleep, the ghost crept to his doorway and stood there, staring at Nathan as he breathed the even breaths of deep sleep.

How does Nathan know the ghost was watching him if he was sleeping? Because one night, some inexplicable sensation woke him suddenly. His startled eyes focused on the ghost framed in the doorway, draped in a trench coat with a hat pulled down over his faceless head. Nothing was visible but the hat and coat, posed in a watching stance.

The next day, Nathan told his brother about his ghostly encounter. During the conversation, either Nathan or, more likely his brother, must have said something that offended the ghost. That night, after the family left the house at 6:00 pm, his brother's rock collection was inexplicably heaved off the table and scattered all over the floor. They found the mess when they returned home after 10:30 pm. No one else had been in the locked house while the family was away. Nothing was missing. The rocks were spread far and wide, not just piled in a heap as if they'd simply fallen to the floor. "Unlike me, my brother is not a firm believer in ghost," Nathan explains.

The trench coat ghost must have decided that Nathan needed watching even when he wasn't asleep, because Nathan felt it form an invisible attachment to him. He was certain it was watching him even when he couldn't see it, and was aware if it following him around.

The haunting stopped when his family moved away from the possessed house, leaving the ghost behind to watch an empty room.

What made the washing machine lid open and close during the spin cycle when no one was near it? Was there actually the spirit of a repairman or washer woman from days gone by marveling at the new invention?

Who was the ghost in the trench coat? Was he a spy guarding secrets in the old house? Did he get revenge when Nathan's brother got too close to some old truth? Why did it attach to Nathan? Could he have resembled the ghost's last contact in mortality?

A Difference of Opinion

It wasn't until she was sixteen that Michelle D'Ambrosio finally got a room of her own. Every other place she'd lived had been houses or apartments so small that she'd had to share a room with her little brother. At last her family had a house with enough rooms that one was for her alone, and she could hardly wait to set it up just the way she wanted it.

Michelle eagerly placed her bed, dresser, and chair in just the right places, then arranged her stuffed animals, clothes, and shoes. As she surveyed her handiwork one last time before falling asleep that night, she felt a gratifying sense of control over her own space.

The next morning, she got ready for school and shut the door behind her with a satisfying *click*. Everything was right with the world.

Yet when she returned home and opened her bedroom door, she stared in disbelief at the rearranged furniture. Who had come in and moved her bed, dresser, and chair? Who'd thrown her stuffed animals in the closet and pulled some of her clothes off the hangers?

Michelle immediately confronted her family, but none of them admitted to moving any of her things. They seemed sincerely shocked at her news. When they went to see the room for themselves. Michelle couldn't find a guilty gleam in anyone's eye.

While her mother helped Michelle move her furniture back in place, she explained that she'd been at work all day, and couldn't think of any reason anyone would want to take the trouble to move Michelle's furniture around. Once everything was back in place, her mother sat on Michelle's bed and asked, "Did I tell you about Opa?"

Michelle thought of her cigar-smoking Dutch grandfather, from whom her mother had inherited the china hutch downstairs. "What about him?"

"Well, there are times when I'm near the hutch and feel as if he's there. Then I'll smell his cigars and know that he's checking up on me. He's my Guardian Angel, Michelle. He's here to protect me, and you, too, from evil or harm."

Michelle's eyebrows rose. "Do you think he's moving my furniture?"

Her mother laughed. "I don't know why he would."

Then next day when Michelle returned home, she opened her door with anxious anticipation, but to her relief, everything was as she'd left it that morning.

A couple of days later, Michelle was taken by surprise to find her furniture again moved back to the unwanted positions. With determination, she put her things back where she wanted them, fished her stuffed animals out of the closet, and hung up her clothes.

From then on, Michelle's furniture would stay as she'd arranged it for a little while, but every so often would shift back to someone else's idea of how the room should look.

Could one of Michelle's family members have been playing a prank on her? Could it have been her visiting grandfather's spirit rearranging her things the way he thought they should be? Or was there another spirit, perhaps a teenage girl from an earlier time, who thought the furniture should be arranged as hers was when she was alive...the "right" way?

Guests in the Graveyard

Aaron Worrell's lifelong interest in ghosts may be a family trait that extends to his two older brothers. Before Aaron was born, his brother, Michael, refused to sleep by himself, claiming that some guy pushed him down in the toy room. The culprit wasn't four-year-old Michael's older brother, Joey, who has Down syndrome. Michael was more than happy to be with Joey, in spite of his habit of stopping play once in awhile to say something in the direction of the toy room window. His speech wasn't clear, but it was obvious he was carrying on a conversation.

The boys' mother, Carolyn, has no doubt that Joey sees things other people can't, adding, "Sometimes he'll tell them, 'Hush.'"

When Joey was sixteen, Michael ten, and Aaron four, the family moved to Manti, Utah, where Michael watched his toys slide around the floor on their own as if invisible little hands were playing with them. No one seemed to believe his story about the moving toys, perhaps because he and Joey were the only ones who saw it happen, and Joey wasn't telling.

Besides the invisible playmates, Michael watched a transparent man walk past the bottom of the stairs into a bedroom. Later, Michael saw the same man standing on the staircase.

The house also offered a strange sight to Aaron, who was too young to accurately describe the strange beings he saw from his bed one night.

He has a vague memory of claiming that he saw little white deers. No one else could see them, but when his mother asked why he called what he saw "deers," he said they had horns. Carolyn's impression was that the horned beings were up to no good, so the family was happy to move away from that house.

When Aaron got to high school, he met Phoenix and Caleb, who also had an interest in the occult. The three of them eagerly planned ghost-hunting trips to area graveyards.

First they made a ghost box out of a radio, tampering with it until it continuously scanned through bands of white noise. Then they waited until dark on various nights before setting out to see what they could find.

In nearby Sterling, the amateur ghost hunters didn't hear anything among the tombstones. A bit further south in Mayfield, they got a little bit of activity from the cemetery. Their next destination was a mile north of Ephraim where they got the words, "…watching you…" in an old abandoned pioneer cemetery. Sensing that the spirits there were scared of the flesh and blood intruders, they didn't stay long.

According to Aaron, the voices filtering through the ghost box have distinctive sounds, ranging from deep, rough words to higher pitched women's tones, and even children's voices.

Once the intrepid hunters hit the Manti Cemetery at 1:00 a.m. on a dark, moonless night, they encountered the most activity of all.

Although they've seen orbs in various places, they watched a yellow orb move in a deliberate line from one gravestone to behind another and disappear. In the ghost-hunting world, yellow is a color of warning.

As soon as Phoenix turned on the ghost box, the hunters asked, "Is there anyone here?"

The name "John" came through the static.

"Where are you buried, John?"

"Thirty steps."

With a camera rolling, the boys counted thirty steps forward, and then trained their video camera on the surrounding headstones. The first name, "John," was spotted right away.

The trio soon discovered that the west edge of the cemetery near the statue of a woman produced a lot of activity. Aaron says that if someone walks around the statue three times and says the right words, the statue will cry. Not knowing the words, he's never tried it, but their camera stopped working in statue's shadow. In spite of fresh batteries, Phoenix's flashlight also went dark with the stone woman looking over his shoulder.

When the boys returned to the cemetery on another night, they asked if whoever was there remembered them. A voice through the ghost box said, "Aaron...Aaron...Aaron."

Aaron wasn't surprised to hear his name, because every time they've returned, the spirits remember the boys. Even the word, "hieroglyphics" that came through the ghost box makes sense, since Aaron has a tattoo of pyramids and an Egyptian-styled All-Seeing Eye on his forearm.

There were other more ominous messages from the ghost box.

"Be careful."

"Bad here."

"Demon."

Right after the warnings, a new gravelly voice said, "Leave now. Come back later."

The boys obeyed, leaving the cemetery at 2:30 am and not returning until the "witching hour" at 3:00 am. That's when they encountered a presence claiming to be another entity, yet the gravelly voice was recognizable as the one that told them to return. Through questioning, the ghost hunters determined this was a bad ghost trying to provoke fear in them by growling out evil names and making threats about what they would do to the flesh and blood boys.

When the hunters got home and pulled out a Ouija board, they called up a spirit and asked if it was the one talking to them in the cemetery.

"No."

They asked if the contact knew who was in the cemetery.

"Yes."

The board spelled out the name of a well-known demon throughout history. Aaron won't reveal its name because names have power, and the more one interacts with this demon, the more it influences the person to self-harm or even suicide.

A more benign name revealed from the board is Evesti Koazhee. Claiming to be an Aztec warrior and chief, he's come through more than once. The boys have asked him general questions, such as what the afterlife is like. Evesti tells them what he can, which mostly is that he enjoys it.

Aaron has no concerns about using the Ouija board or tracking down ghosts, since spirits don't scare him. Even though he and his friends haven't gone ghost hunting for a while, he says they'll probably do it again.

What creates the voices that come through the ghost box? Is it something to do with mixed up wiring in a doctored radio? Or are spirits really communicating through the static?
Is the Ouija board just a game with a bad reputation? Or does it actually communicate with spirits of the dead?

Haunted House

The sunset shadows creeping over the 500 acre Yakima, Washington fruit tree farm where Midge lived deepened her fear of coming nightmares that occurred frequently and forced the seven-year-old awake, shaking with fright.

Just before her eighth birthday, Midge woke up in the early morning darkness, too scared to be alone. Hurrying past her two older sisters' closed bedroom doors, she reached her parents' room and crawled in between their sleeping bodies. Staring out their window through the lace curtains, she willed the sun to rise. Midge's life was always better in the light.

Shifting her gaze to the center of the room, Midge noticed the imprint of lace remaining in her vision like a ghost image hanging in the air. With rising dread, Midge watched the faint web of lace begin revolving as the closet door slid open, revealing a dark corner of the closet. To Midge's horror, a long, hot-pink tentacle slid out of the black corner and extended toward her. Recognizing it as a horribly deformed spider's leg, she shut her eyes and buried her face in the blankets, shivering in fear. After a few moments, she peeked over the edge of the covers.

The leg was gone.

As she watched with mounting terror, it extended from the closet toward her again, stretching out as if intending to grab her. Terrified, she hid under the blankets again.

To her immense relief, her father woke up before the spider leg reached her. When he got out of bed to go to the bathroom, Midge followed him as closely as she could, too terrified to stay behind with the horribly mutated spider-thing. Glancing back, she saw a writhing pink snake-like leg following her down the hall.

Nearly paralyzed with fright, she cried, "Daddy, there's a big spider behind me!"

"You're bigger than a spider," Dad growled, the familiar scent of alcohol wafting from his mouth before he turned into the bathroom and shut the door.

Midge threw another fearful glance down the hallway, but the spider was gone.

When Midge told her parents what she'd seen, they said it was just her imagination running away with her. Sensing their impatience, Midge decided it would be better to keep her fears to herself.

Perhaps whatever was after her thought she should keep her mouth shut, too, because there were times when Midge felt as if her open mouth was stuffed full of cobwebs. Innocently sharing this experience for 2nd grade Show and Tell, Midge was surprised when her classmates make fun of her, claiming she made it up just to get attention. That's when Midge came to the lonely realization that she couldn't tell anyone what happened to her and expect them to believe her.

As Midge grew older, she'd awaken in the night with the distinct feeling of evil lurking in the dark corner of her bedroom. She was certain that something wicked was waiting there, watching her.

One stormy night when she was too big to crawl in bed between her parents, Midge became so afraid that her mother finally got into bed with her. This was no sacrifice on her mother's part, since Midge's parents often slept apart after their frequent fights.

In spite of the funny-looking foam hairnet she wore, Mom's presence was so comforting that Midge managed to fall asleep in spite of the rumbling thunder and flashes of lightning.

Suddenly, she snapped awake, her heart pounding in time with the ominous song sung by the witch's guards in the "Wizard of Oz." She couldn't locate the source of the sinister song, but could hear it plainly amid the rolls of thunder.

Midge sat up and stared at her mother, deciding if she should wake her up to ask if she could hear the menacing tune. Yet if Mom couldn't hear it, would she be so annoyed at Midge for waking her up that she'd go back to her own room?

As Midge gazed at her mother with dreadful indecision, she suddenly noticed the foam liner of Mom's hair net peel back, allowing the next lightning flash to give Midge a terrifying glimpse of her mother's skull, the bone bright white against the pillow.

Midge squeezed her eyes shut and huddled against the wall for the rest of the night, trembling as she waited for the sun to rise.

In her teen years, Midge was visiting her grandparents in the house next door when she found a Ouija board in her mother's old bedroom. There were only two houses in the secluded orchard, and she never felt afraid at her grandparents' home. Distressed by her discovery, Midge quickly returned the board to its place, wishing she'd never touched it. If her mother had played with the board, had the spirits she conjured up followed her across the lawn to take up residence in her new house? Were they what made her fall into depression and experience nervous breakdowns?

When Midge left home to go to college, she was relieved to find that she was suddenly free of nightmares. She had such a sensitivity to frightening things that she couldn't watch scary movies, not that she wanted to. She gratefully relaxed into the feeling of complete safety in her dormitory.

On her first visit home for the holidays, Midge was distressed that the nightmares returned. Knowing what it was like to sleep without dread, it was especially hard to endure the old patterns of fearful, sleepless nights.

With a sense of relief, Midge returned to school at the end of her holiday. Soon she met a good, upstanding man named Bruno who lived his religion. When he asked her to marry him, she was happy to say, "Yes."

The day she took him home to meet her family, he was assigned the guest room. After shutting himself in for the night, Midge was washing her face in the bathroom across the hall when she heard a knock on the bathroom door. "Midge?" Bruno called softly.

Midge opened the door to see Bruno glancing over his shoulder at the open door to his room. He turned to face her. "I need to tell you something."

The two of them made their way to the deserted living room, where Midge turned on a lamp and sat beneath its warm glow. Bruno sat beside her. "Now, hear me out before you say anything," he said. "About a minute after I laid down to sleep, it felt like someone sat down on the mattress to my left. The bed actually dipped down from the weight, but when I opened my eyes, I couldn't see anyone. Then something rolled over on top of me." Bruno caught one of Midge's hands as if she could save him from his memories. "I couldn't breathe. I couldn't speak. I thought I was going to die in that room. Then, whatever it was rolled off the bed to the right of me and left."

As Midge stared into Bruno's frightened eyes, an odd mix of fear, empathy, and relief washed through her. For the first time in her life, someone else acknowledged that there was actually something evil in the house. All of her frightening experiences were validated.

Years later, Midge received more confirmation when she read a section in the book, "Embraced by the Light." The description of horrid-looking evil creatures that the author, Betty J. Eadie, saw in her hospital room was so similar to what Midge had seen that it helped her feel as if she wasn't crazy after all. She wasn't the only one who'd seen them.

As an adult, Midge has had experiences with unseen entities. For example, while doing dishes, she's felt a push so hard that she had to catch herself. Then she wonders, *Who are you, and why are you trying to get my attention?*

Midge also discovered her next oldest sister, Mavon, who is seven years older, was listening when Midge tried explaining the scary things she'd seen to their parents. Mavon told Midge that hearing their parents discount her stories made Mavon decide to keep the spooky things she'd experienced to herself. She didn't want her parents thinking she was crazy and saying that it was all in her head. She knew it was real.

Midge's oldest sister, Mary, who's nine years older, never said anything about scary things in the house.

What made Midge's childhood home so frightening? Did it have something to do with the Ouija board she found? Was it because of her mother's nervous breakdowns? Or was it the other way around - did the evil cause her mother's emotional turmoil?

Did her father's alcoholism have anything to do with it? Did the fighting in this unhappy marriage create a spirit of contention that masked their ability to sense the evil in their home?

Happy Birthday Ghost

Midge enjoyed growing up next door to her fun-loving maternal grandfather. They were the only two neighbors in sight, since their houses were built on Grandpa's 500 acre fruit tree farm. Grandpa's child-like enthusiasm made holidays and birthdays very special for Midge and her two older sisters. It seems that even after he passed away, Grandpa's big-kid-at-heart spirit came back to visit Midge on her birthday, December 5, 1995.

Decorating the Christmas tree at her Arizona home while listening to her children giggle over her birthday surprises in the kitchen, Midge picked up an extra special ornament. It was pretty enough as it was, but when it was turned on, it was spectacular. Not only did it light up, but it played the beautiful "Greensleeves" melody and revolved all at the same time. After placing it on a branch, she turned it on. Instead of the light and music show, there was nothing. After trying everything she could think of, and having her husband try everything he could think of to make it work, Midge was disappointed that it didn't light up. She decided to leave it on the tree anyway, telling herself she would remember what it looked and sounded like in its full glory.

After the candles were blown out on her birthday cake, the ice cream eaten, and her presents opened, everyone hugged her "goodnight" and went to bed.

Midge decided to stay up for awhile. Feeling nostalgic, she sat on the floor in the dim living room, watching the lights glow among the Christmas tree branches and thinking of how special Grandpa had made her feel on her birthdays. Then, without warning, the special ornament lit up and revolved in a slow circle while the notes of "Greensleeves" filled the air. Midge could hardly believe what she was seeing. A flood of warmth filled her heart as tears rose in her eyes. Grandpa was in the room with her. Wrapping her arms around her shoulders, she reveled in the feeling of his love and the magical movement of her special ornament.

After a time, Midge's eyes grew heavy as she watched the mesmerizing spectacle. At last, she whispered, "Thank you, Grandpa. I love you." Then she went to sleep.

The ornament never worked again.

By the time Midge reached her birthday on December 5, 2014, she had acquired a book-shaped music box titled, "The Nutcracker." The "Dance of the Sugar Plum Fairy" wouldn't play unless the box was opened just like a book. Along with the classic melody, a miniature Clara figurine whirled around inside the book with a nutcracker in her arms.

Midge kept the music box on her bookshelf. It was safely tucked away when she went to sleep on the night of December 4.

At 5:00 am on her birthday, Midge got an unexpected wake-up call when her music box blasted "Dance of the Sugar Plum Fairy," bringing her and her husband awake. As her husband jumped out of bed and rushed over to the shelf to close the book, Midge said, "It has to be Grandpa wishing me a happy birthday, but I don't appreciate him doing it so early in the morning!"

Could a loose wire in the ornament have connected somehow while Midge was watching the tree late at night? Or did her grandfather actually come to keep her company on her birthday, fixing an obstinate ornament as his gift to her?

Since Midge and her husband were the only ones living in the house, who opened the music box book while they were asleep? Did it somehow fall open? Or did Grandpa do it so Midge would know that he was still celebrating her birthday with her?

Neat Freak Nanny

Even though Beverly and her friend, Karla, both lived at the Fort Riley, Kansas, Army Base, their houses were not the same. For one thing, Karla's was the largest house on General's Row. Beverly discovered an even bigger difference when she took her children to Karla's to help her get ready for a Christmas party.

As the children unwrapped fragile Christmas tree decorations from protective paper before hanging them on the pine tree, Beverly and Karla worked in the kitchen, finishing up the party food. As soon as the children completed their holiday task, they left the living room in a noisy group to go play with toys.

Over the sound of her knife chopping crab for wonton ragoons, Beverly heard paper rustling in the front room. She stopped, head cocked toward the doorway. "It sounds like the kids are still decorating, but I thought they were done." After a moment, she added, "It sounds like they're having a paper fight." Setting her knife down, she said, "I'd better go stop them."

That's when she noticed an odd look on Karla's face, and heard her murmur in her rich German accent, "They must have left the papers out." Turning toward the doorway, Karla called, "Leave it alone! I'll take care of it when I get my cooking done."

The rustling abruptly stopped.

"I'll go talk to them," Beverly said, determined that her children would help clean up.

Beverly's daughter, Carolyn, suddenly appeared in the doorway, her eyes wide with worry. "Mom? Papers were flying around the living room just now."

Beverly sighed. "You kids don't have to make a bigger mess, you know. Just put all the papers back in the decoration boxes."

Carolyn's gaze flicked to Karla at the stove, then back to her mother. "But, Mom, it wasn't us. No one was in there when the papers were flying all over the place."

Embarrassed, Beverly turned toward Karla to apologize, but stopped in confusion when she saw her friend nodding in agreement. "I know you didn't do it," Karla said to Carolyn. "It's all right. Go back to playing."

As Carolyn disappeared down the hallway, Beverly asked, "What was that about?"

"Well," Karla said, dropping a wonton into a pan to test the oil's heat, "I have a ghost."

Beverly laughed, but Karla's expression remained somber. "It is a lady ghost who likes things neat and tidy. I call her the Neat Freak Nanny. I have to keep my house very clean every day if I don't want to anger her. If she's upset, the mess can get worse. I do my best to keep quiet about her, because I don't want everyone to know I have a ghost."

Beverly couldn't imagine Karla making jokes about being haunted. Not only did she come from a no-nonsense German background, she was married to the Lieutenant Colonel Post Commander. "It is not all bad," Karla confided, scooping the golden fried wonton out of the oil. "The ghost is not just a fastidious housekeeper, she is also a protector. "

"How?" Beverly was genuinely curious.

"For one thing, she will not let my children sleep with their bedroom door closed. I closed their door at night when we first moved in, but the door opened by itself. I suspected the boys were sneaking out of bed, but when I checked, they were sound asleep. No matter how many times I closed the door, it would always open by itself. Now I just leave it that way." She scooped up several wontons and dropped them into the oil, where they sizzled, releasing the delicious warm scent of frying dough.

"I wonder," Beverly said carefully, "If you have a ghost, do you think something bad happened to her children with their door closed, and she doesn't want the same thing to happen to yours?"

Karla turned her head and lowered her brows. "*If* I have a ghost?"

Beverly shrugged.

Karla turned back to her cooking. "Perhaps. I don't know much about her, except that she lets me know when something is wrong." She stirred the crackling wontons as Beverly mixed more savory filling.

"How?"

"Sometimes she gets really noisy if things aren't right." Karla glanced back at Beverly. "If you spend time here, you will see."

Karla scooped wontons out of the oil, holding the slotted spoon over the pan as oil drained off the crispy Chinese dumplings. "If someone comes who is not a good person, I can tell by how the ghost acts. Then I know not to trust that person. She has never been wrong."

Over her next few visits, Beverly noticed occasional strange noises in Karla's house, such as unexplained clicking sounds, doors creaking when no one was near them, and sounds like soft footfalls crossing the floor.

Not long after Karla had a baby, she called Beverly and asked if she would please come over to help clean. "I've been so tired," Karla explained. "The Neat Freak Nanny is upset about the state of the house, but I need to rest."

Beverly gathered her children and hurried over to Karla's house. After making Karla sit down with her baby, she got her older girls washing dishes while Carolyn pulled out the vacuum cleaner.

"I'll clean the baby's room," Beverly offered.

"You don't need to."

"I don't mind," Beverly assured Karla. "After that, I'll clean the bathroom."

Karla shook her head. "You don't understand. The baby's room never gets dirty. His clothes are always put away, his blankets don't stay rumpled, the floor is clean, and there's never a speck of dust or smudged window."

Beverly stared at her. "How can that be?"

Karla gave her a tired smile. "We wondered the same thing, so we put a video camera in there. Here, I'll show you." Karla retrieved the camera, then sat down and patted the sofa cushion beside her. Beverly sat down and watched Karla back away from the camera, then bend over the crib to pick up her baby. Pushing a stack of folded baby clothes aside, she laid her baby down and changed him, then carried him from the room.

"Let me fast forward." Karla advanced the film. When it stopped, Beverly stared in amazement at the crib blanket twitching. Then, ever so slowly, it inched up over the mattress, appearing to move of its own accord as it stretched into a smooth plane. Next, the diaper fell from the changing table into the garbage can. Then the dresser drawer inched open, the clean stack of baby clothes toppled into the drawer, and it slowly slid shut. In the now-tidy room, the empty rocking chair tipped back and forth, back and forth.

Who is the Neat Freak Nanny? Is she the wife of some long-ago post commander who still adheres to a rigidly clean military-style environment?
Why is the baby's room always clean? Was that where the spirit kept her baby? Or was that her own quiet space that she still keeps peaceful and spotless?

Ghostly Footprints

Beverly might have been more surprised by Karla's ghost if her mother hadn't had a strange experience. Born in 1919, Beverly's mother, Lois, grew into a young woman who imagined what her first home would be like, but she never imagined it would come with a ghost.

When Lois met Merrill Smith, she was quite taken with the sturdy young man who got a steady job with the U.S. Post Office. When he asked her to marry him, she said, "Yes!" The new Mr. and Mrs. Smith happily set up residence in a "shotgun house" on Short Street in Kansas City, Kansas. A shotgun house is one where a person can stand at the front door and look straight through the house out the back door.

One afternoon, Lois was sitting on the bed when she felt a strange sensation. The bed moved, almost as if it were taking big breaths.The thought flashed through Lois's mind, *Is there a tornado?* But that didn't make any sense. There wasn't any wind, only late yellow sunlight slanting through the window. *Was it an earthquake?*

When Lois stood up, the house went still. Had the earthquake stopped? Lois looked around for any evidence of damage. That's when she saw the impression of two little feet pressing into the bed, then releasing… pressing in, releasing. There was no one in sight, just the impression of a pair of feet there, then gone, there, then gone. A cold shudder slid around beneath Lois's skin.

Lois ran from the room toward the front door, nearly running into Merrill coming home. With a grin, Merrill said, "I'm glad to see you, too!"

"Come…here," Lois gasped.

Merrill took hold of Lois's arm as if he were afraid she might fall over. "Are you all right?"

"You have to see." She pulled him toward the bedroom and stood in the doorway, staring at the smooth spread on the bed.

Merrill looked over her head into the room. "It looks nice," he said carefully. "New curtains?"

Lois shook her head. "No! There was… something… I don't know what… jumping on the bed."

"Was it a spider?" Merrill walked into the room, inspecting the bed while unbuttoning his uniform. "Do you want me to kill it? You find it while I get changed, then I'll swat it for you."

"Not a spider!" Lois cried. "I saw… I don't know… little dents pushing down in the mattress, then letting up, as if… don't laugh… someone was jumping on the bed."

Merrill didn't reply as he changed out of his postman uniform.

"I really saw it, Merrill," Lois paused to twist a lock of her hair, "but now it's gone."

"All right," Merrill said, giving her an affectionate pat. "If it happens again, come and get me." He went out to the living room to read the newspaper.

After a few days with no strange activity, Lois began relaxing as she entered the bedroom. Could the strange dents have somehow been made by mice under the covers? The thought made her shudder, but not as much as having an invisible someone jumping up and down on her bed.

Then one day as Lois carried an armload of laundry into the bedroom, she heard a faint, rhythmic sound. As she peered around the folded clothes, she saw the dreaded little footprints pressing themselves into the mattress, then letting up, then pressing in.

She stood paralyzed for a moment before backing out of the room. She set the laundry on the couch. Merrill wouldn't be home for a couple of hours. Would it keep going long enough for him to see?

Maybe not.

Lois twisted her hair. Suddenly she stopped twisting and dashed to the closet for the camera. She wasn't very good at photography, but any picture was better than none.

Lois carried the camera to the bedroom. From the doorway, she stared at the smooth bed. No footprints. Surprised at her disappointment, Lois carried the camera back to the closet. Should she tell Merrill what she'd seen when he got home? Would he believe her?

She told him. Merrill took another look in the bedroom, pressing his fingers to the bed, then lifting the cover and looking underneath. "Well," he said, "hopefully the next time it happens, I'll be home."

Lois loved that guy.

A week later, Lois followed Merrill into the bedroom and sat on the bed to talk to him while he changed. Thats when she felt the familiar up and down movement on the mattress. Before she could say anything, Merrill stopped and asked, "What is that?"

Lois jumped up. "It's what I've been telling you about," she said, pointing to the little dents going in and out of the mattress. "Something's jumping on the bed."

"Okay." Merrill gently took hold of Lois and pulled her from the room, his eyes wandering back to the footprints appearing and disappearing in the blanket. "We are going to talk to the landlord."

When the landlord answered the door, Merrill got right to the point. "Earl, we want to know the history of the house we're renting from you."

It turned out that a little girl had died in that house.

When Merrill and Lois got back home, they knelt together and prayed for the girl. They said she was not where she belonged, and asked for some heavenly presence to come and get her.

After that, there were no more incidents of feet-shaped dents in the bed.

Ghostly feet seem to run in the family, since Lois's daughter, Beverly, also had an encounter with disembodied feet.

It happened while her husband was stationed at Fort Riley, Kansas. When a new family moved onto base, Beverly and several other military wives and their husbands helped the newcomers move in.

While the guys tried to get the basement storm doors open to haul in appliances, the women took over the inside of the house, vacuuming carpet and wiping out cupboards before unpacking dishes. Since the kitchen was just above the basement doors, the women entertained themselves by periodically looking out the window to assess their husbands' progress.

Since none of the mens' efforts could budge the doors, they ultimately decided to go to the hardware store for tools to pry them open. The men drove away and the women kept working.

Suddenly, the tramp of Army boots sounded on the staircase leading down from the second story of the house. The footfalls rounded the corner in the stairwell and continuing down to the basement.

The women looked at each other in puzzlement. Had the men returned? How could they have gotten upstairs undetected? Glancing out the window as the sound of tromping boots moved across the basement floor, the women saw that the vehicle had not returned.

One brave soul edged toward the stairs and stuck her head around the doorjamb to check the basement. A loud *crash* made her shriek and scurry back to the huddle of women in the kitchen.

"Well," the woman closest to the window said a bit breathlessly, "at least the basement doors are open."

The women all turned to the window and saw that it was true. Hurrying outside to see who had accomplished the difficult task, as well as scold whoever it was for giving them such a scare, they stopped in confusion at the open doors.

There was no one there.

All the men returned in the vehicle. None of them had stayed behind.

What created the rhythmic impressions in the mattress that Lois and Merrill both saw? What could have made them except for the ghost of a little girl who'd died in the house, and was at last free to jump on the bed without reproach because no one could see her doing it?

How did the doors spontaneously burst open at a house in Fort Riley when several men couldn't get them apart with their combined strength? What created the sound of booted feet tromping on stairs? Could the ghost of a former tenant feel contempt that the soldiers couldn't open doors that it could break free with just one shove?

Texts From the Grave

Carolyn Teasdale not only got a great husband when she married Richard, she also developed a close, loving relationship with his Grandma Tracy. Not only was this lady fun to be around, but she shared Carolyn's passion for family history. The two of them spent many happy hours together tracking their ancestors, which served to deepened their bond.

One day in early autumn, Carolyn was delighted to tell her grandmother, "Grandma, I'm going to have a baby."

Grandma Tracy's eyes brightened as she pulled Carolyn into a hug. "That's wonderful! When is she coming?"

Carolyn laughed. "We don't know if it's a girl or boy yet." She pulled away to look into Grandma's eyes, "But the baby is due in April."

Grandma clapped her hands. "That's a perfect time to have a baby. It's when I had my Kris, you know," she said, using her nickname for Carolyn's mother-in-law, Kristyl. "I can't wait to meet your baby girl! I've got to tell my friends." As Grandma pulled out her mobile phone and began texting, Carolyn decided not to stop Grandma from announcing the future arrival of a baby girl. She had a 50% chance of guessing the baby's gender right, and if she was wrong, she'd just have to correct herself.

No one knew that Grandma wouldn't get the chance to be proven right or wrong before her sudden death on December 17.

Although Grandma was sorely missed, life went on after the funeral. Carolyn and Richard eventually welcomed their baby daughter on Kristyl's birthday, April 3. Before they could even let their parents know that little Gwynneth had arrived, Kris called. When Richard put his mother on speaker, Carolyn couldn't miss the excitement in her voice. "You won't believe what just happened! I got a text from Mom!"

Momentarily confused, Carolyn wondered who she was talking about. Not Grandma Tracy, of course, so who did Kris think texted her? Before Carolyn could figure out a reasonable explanation, Kris continued, "The message says, 'Happy Birthday! Did you get my gift? She has a great middle name.'"

Stunned, Carolyn turned to stare at her husband, who returned her bewildered look. Only the two of them knew they'd just chosen Grandma's maiden name, Hannah, as Gwynneth's middle name, and had both agreed to reveal it to the family later on.

"Did you…?" Carolyn asked.

Richard shook his head, hands up in self-defense. "It wasn't me."

Kristyl's next words broke Carolyn's jumbled thoughts apart. "I didn't tell you that my sister Valerie got a text from Mom two weeks ago," she said. Valerie's young daughter, Brenda, suffered from a personality disorder that resulted in her throwing fits during tense situations. "You see, Brenda was throwing a fit while Valerie was getting ready to host a party, but Valerie was too busy to deal with it. She decided to deal with Brenda after she got the jello mold in the refrigerator. That's when she got a text from Mom's phone number." Kristyl's voice dropped. "It said to go check on Brenda now. Valerie was so startled that she hurried out of the kitchen and found Brenda rolling on the floor, clutching her stomach and screaming. That wasn't her ordinary behavior, so Valerie took her to the doctor."

"I remember," Carolyn said. "She had appendicitis."

"Her appendix had burst," Kristyl said.

Carolyn glanced at Richard. "I didn't know about the text, though."

"Not many people did," Kristyl answered. "You must admit, it's rather hard to believe. But now I got one, too!"

Although it was discussed more than once, no one could explain the text messages sent from a dead woman's phone number.

The mystery didn't end there. When Gwynneth was three years old, her mother scolded her, asking why she was pestering her sister, Rachel.

Gwynn deflected the question with one of her own. "Where's Grandma and the guy?"

Frustrated at her daughter's attempt to shift the conversation, Carolyn glanced at her mother, Beverly, who was visiting. Grandpa hadn't come, so Gwynn's question about Grandma and the guy made no sense. The little girl's speech was indistinct enough that it was possible she'd said, "Grandma in disguise," but that didn't make sense, either.

Beverly raised her eyebrows as if to say, *She's your daughter. You handle it.*

Carolyn turned back to Gwynn and said firmly, "What I asked is why you were bothering Rachel."

Gwynn's little face scrunched up into worry lines as she looked out the window and repeated, "Where's Grandma and the guy?"

Thinking that brief acknowledgment might steer the conversation back on track, Carolyn gave a quick nod toward her mother. "Grandma's right there, and she's not with a guy."

Gwynn sighed deeply, as if trying to explain something to an adult was a burden. Turning to her mother, she over-enunciated, "No! Not that grandma! Grandma - in - duh - sky!" She pointed upward out the window.

Mystified, Carolyn decided to try to understand what her daughter was saying. "What color is Grandma in the sky's hair?"

"Black."

Knowing that Gwynn had confused black, brown, and gray in the past, Carolyn asked what color her own brown hair was.

"Black."

With no black-haired grandmothers besides Beverly, who was definitely not "Grandma in the sky," Carolyn asked, "When did you see her, Gwynnie?"

The little girl shook her head longingly. "Not today."

Choosing her words carefully, Carolyn asked, "Did you see her in a dream?"

"NO!" came the immediate answer. "I was playing."

"Did you see this grandma today or another day?"

"Another day."

Checking to see if Gwynn was simply repeating the last thing she heard, Carolyn rephrased her question. "Did you see her another day, or today?"

The child's expression drooped into sadness. "She didn't see me today. When is she going to see me again?"

A chill ran through Carolyn. Grasping at any explanation, she asked, "Are you talking about your friend's grandmas, or your other grandmas?"

Gwynn squeezed her hands into little fists and jutted out her chin. "No!"

Since each question only made Gwynn more distressed, Carolyn scrolled through two generation's worth of pictures on the computer, including step-grandmas, both alive and deceased.

When Grandma Tracy's gray-haired picture came up, Gwynn did not react. The next photo showed Grandma and Grandpa Tracy in their early married years, grinning at the camera with their arms around each other. Gwynn bounced up and down, pointing to the smiling face of her dark-haired great grandmother. "There she is! There's Grandma in the sky!"

A shiver ran up Carolyn's arms. "Where have you seen Grandma in the sky?"

The little girl returned to the window that offered an exceptional view of Squaw Peak. Leaning way over, she pointed north. "Grandma in the sky lives on the mountain, and in the sky." Her little finger held steady in the direction of East Lawn Cemetery - Grandma Tracy's burial place. Gwynn dropped her hand and gave her mother a radiant smile. "She says 'Hi' to me."

Gwynn hadn't been to the cemetery for two years, not since she'd been learning to walk.

Balancing on a fine line between fascination and the heebie jeebies, Carolyn asked, "What else does Grandma in the sky say to you?"

Gwynn put her hands out to either side of her small body as if making an onstage announcement. "She says we needs to find her Mommies and Daddies."

Carolyn was speechless. Apparently, she needed to do more genealogy. The thought also occurred to her that the name "Hannah" seemed very appropriate for her daughter, who appeared to have an even greater connection with her Great-grandma Tracy than a shared name.

On Memorial Day, Gwynneth drew a picture for Grandma in the sky before climbing in the van to visit her grave. They met extended family, including Grandma Kristyl, at East Lawn Cemetery. As they put flowers on the graves, they talked about their loved ones buried there.

While riding home, Gwynn twisted in her car seat to look out the back window. Turning forward, she said, "Grandma in the sky's not following us." In the moment of surprised silence following her announcement, she glanced around the inside of the van, then declared, "She's not in the car, either."

When her sister, Katie, asked, "Did you see Grandma in the sky at the cemetery?" Not wanting to encourage Gwynn to make things up about Grandma Tracy, Carolyn gave Katie a warning look. But without further prompting, Katie's question brought more information. "Grandma in the sky was very happy we went to see her on the mountain," Gwynn said, bobbing her head with excitement. While there'd been talk about Grandma Tracy at the cemetery, no one had mentioned, "Grandma in the sky." Then Gwynn stilled her little body, tipped her head, and asked, "Mommy, who's Kris?"

Carolyn was so startled, she nearly ran off the road. She'd never heard anyone call her mother-in-law "Kris," except Grandma Tracy.

"Grandma in the sky came to visit Kris, too," Gwynn announced.

"Gwynnie," Carolyn asked gently, "What else did you see and hear with Grandma in the sky?"

Staring out the window, Gwynn answered, "Grandma in the sky fell on the mountain. That's why she lays down there. She is on two mountains. One is a white mountain. She doesn't lay on that one. She falls down on that mountain and hurts her knees."

"How does she hurt her knees?" Carolyn asked softly.

After letting out a sigh bigger than she was, the little girl explained, "Grandma goes to the mountain and falls on her knees and cries, so her knees must hurt."

"Why does she cry?"

"Grandma in the sky cries because her family won't stop crying." Gwynn turned away from the window and pointed to herself. "She wants Gwynnie to show her how Gwynnie can be on her knees too... with Rachel." She dropped her hand. "Grandma in the sky says I don't get to go to the white mountain, but I need to cry on my knees too... with Rachel." A warm smile blossomed across the child's face as she wrapped her arms around herself. "She holds us sometimes."

Through a welling up of emotion, Carolyn asked, "Is the white mountain the temple?"

"No," Gwynn said. "It's just where Grandma in

the sky lives, but not where she lays down." Her big eyes fastened on her mother. "She liked that we came to visit her, Mom. She held us there."

When she got home, Carolyn wrote down all the things that Gwynnie had said. When she shared the information with Kristyl, her mother-in-law was so touched that she shared the stories with everyone in her family.

When Kristyl's estranged siblings read the messages, they felt such a warmth of emotion from Gwynn's stories that they re-established regular contact with their family. Since making up their differences, now when things get tense, the family works it out. No one cuts off communication like they did in the past.

Once everyone was reunited, Gwynn stopped talking about Grandma in the sky.

How did Grandma know Gwynneth would be a girl even before the medical profession could tell? Was it just a lucky 50% guess?

How in the world could Grandma's mobile phone send poignant texts after she died? Was it an abnormal glitch in the airwaves that somehow delayed messages composed while she was alive? If so, how was it possible that she sent congratulations the day of Gwynneth's birth?

And how did a three-year-old come up with her grandmother's nickname of "Kris" when she'd never heard it? How did she recognize a picture of Grandma Tracy? Had the two of them met somewhere between this life and the next, swapping stories in that mysterious space between coming and going?

Looking in the Window

Five nights a week, 51-year-old Gem worked the graveyard shift at an all night convenience store and gas station. The location at an old west crossroads was perfect for tourists, who stopped in at all hours for forgotten toothbrushes, drinks, or snacks for their late night parties. Books at the register entertained visitors with tales of gunfights from a hundred years or more ago, staining the dirt of the crossroads red with blood. Other legends told of cattle drivers drinking themselves to an early death by falling beneath stampeding hooves as cattle raced to the dilapidated pens just outside of town. Most of the old corral fencing had been scavenged by ranchers, or campers for hot dog roasts.

Gem kept busy during the dark hours of her shift by cleaning floors, dusting merchandise, and stocking shelves between customers. They were few and far between in the cold months. The locals sometimes stopped in at night if their child suddenly developed a fever, if they unexpectedly ran out of milk, or had a late night hankering for ice cream.

Gem never noticed anything spooky about her graveyard shift until the night of the storm.

Bruised autumn leaves tore free from their sheltering branches, spinning into the grip of cold winds tossing them in wild circles, ripping, beating them down to the ground to skitter up against the dumpster in twisted agony.

Chilled, Gem wiped the counters around the hot food section before moving over to the checkout counter to straighten the cigarette lighters. That's where she felt eyes on her.

She turned toward the front door to see who her customer was.

No one was there.

Hard rain joined the wind like a slap, flinging icy drops against the glass door, obscuring Gem's vision of the parking lot. But she still felt the eyes. As she stared out into the darkness, she suddenly noticed that the rain seemed to cascade down a vague figure standing just outside the doors. It was gray, almost invisible, appearing to be hunched against the onslaught of rain as it curved around sloped shoulders. The faint image of a broad hat shedding a thin steam of water off the brim hovered over the thing.

Heart pounding like galloping hooves, Gem retreated behind the counter and put the register between her and the door like a shield. When she looked again, she could no longer see the vague form, but her hair stood out as if she'd stuck her finger in the ice cream machine socket.

When Harold Toomey walked in a couple of minutes later, Gem jumped. Shaking the water off his coat, Harold boomed, "It's not a fit night out for man nor beast."

Gem pressed a hand to her careening heart. "Hey, Harold. Did you see anyone else out there just now?"

"No. And I wouldn't be here, either, if Virginia hadn't insisted that she needs cold medicine." Harold spread his hands, silently asking for validation. "If she'd just go to sleep, she wouldn't know she had a cold, now, would she?"

"Oh," Gem said, trying to sound casual. "I just thought I saw someone looking in the window a minute ago."

"Maybe you fell asleep and imagined it. This stuff'll bring out the nightmares in anyone." He gestured toward the storm on the other side of the door with his shoulder.

After Harold left, Gem hovered around the cash register, chiding herself for being so afraid of nothing. She should clean up the water Harold tracked in. With long, confident strides, she headed for the back room, then rolled the bucket and mop out to the main floor. She began mopping at the counter and moved toward the door, following Harold's trail backwards. Just short of the doors, her skin suddenly chilled, sending a tremor across her shoulders.

Eyes on her.

She stumbled backward, glancing wildly around. Had someone come in while she was in the back room? She couldn't see anyone.

"Is anyone here?"

Was that a faint shuffle of a worn cowboy boot in the next aisle over?

Holding her mop as a weapon, Gem rounded the end of the display case and stared down the aisle at nothing. She felt someone there. Someone watching her.

"You don't belong here!" Gem shouted, the mop trembling in her hands.

Eyes on her.

"You're not real!"

Eyes. On. Her.

In a scream that rattled the yogurt machine, Gem shrieked, "Go away!"

A shuffling sound. A whisp of cold air. A ghostly hint of wet manure. Then it was gone. Gem couldn't say how she knew, but the eyes were no longer watching her. Nothing was in the store except her.

Gem remained alone until morning, when she welcomed the sunrise and her replacement cashier.

So far, she's never again felt disembodied eyes on her while working.

What created Gem's feeling of eyes on her? Did the storm's change of atmospheric pressure make her imagine things? If there really was something there, what was it? Could it have been an old cowboy coming back on the hundredth anniversary of his death at the crossroads, surprised to find a building that hadn't been there when he bled his life out on the street?

Ghost Hunting Kit

When the elementary school administration announced his name as a prizewinner, Carson Lawrence hurried to the table to look over the delightful jumble of choices. Drawn to kits that offered a chance to excavate fake dinosaur bones, build your own pyramid, or hunt ghosts, Carson ultimately picked up the ghost hunting kit and carried it home.

When his cousin, Jeffery, came for a sleepover, the two boys commandeered the basement while their mothers, who are sisters, chatted upstairs. The boys eagerly opened the kit, admiring the compass, thermometer, and electrical cable with an attached light bulb. The illustrated instruction book included useful information such as detecting when a ghost's in the area by the thermometer's drop in temperature, the compass pinging rapidly, and the light randomly flicking on and off.

The boys were having so much fun that it was with sudden urgency that they both realized they had to use the bathroom. Now. With a slight head start, Jeffery made a dash for the downstairs bathroom. Knowing his cousin would reach it first, Carson didn't try to beat him, but raced upstairs to second bathroom.

When Carson thundered back down the stairs, his sneakers touched the carpeted floor just as Jeffrey's footsteps sounded from the direction of the bathroom down the hall. As soon as Jeffery spied Carson, he called, "Guess what?"

"What?"

"The toilet paper fell down!"

154

"So?"

"So, it was weird," Jeffery said, looking genuinely frightened. "I think it might have been haunted."

"Haunted toilet paper?" Carson scoffed. "Really? That's so weird. Come on, let's do some experiments."

Both boys turned at the same time, ready to become real ghost hunters. Instead of getting back to their experiments, they stared in bewilderment at the spilled kit. "Did you do this?" Carson demanded, sweeping his arm around the room to indicate the pieces of ghost hunting equipment scattered all over the floor.

"How could I?" Jeffery protested. "You got here before I did!"

It was true.

"I told you there was a ghost," Jeffery said. "It must have tossed the toilet paper off the roller after it trashed your kit. Let's ask him." Jeffery turned toward the center of the room and raised his hands, palms forward. "If you can hear us," he said, his voice deadly serious, "make the light go out."

At that moment, the light fixture flickered and made strange sputtering noises, *pft, pft, pft.*

"Stop it!" Carson whispered. "You're making me paranoid."

The sound of his mother's voice calling down the stairs made Carson jump and Jeffery let out a squeak of fear. "What are you doing down there?"

"Just playing," Carson replied.

"Come on up for a bedtime snack."

"After we put stuff away," Carson called back.

When they gathered up all the pieces of the kit that they could see, Jeffery was unnerved to discover that the instruction book was missing. Searching diligently, he finally found it clear across the room by the fireplace and went ballistic, ripping the book in half.

Carson was willing to give up his spooky kit, so the boys carried all the pieces to the dumpster. As soon as the kit piled on the dumpster floor, the power in the house went out. There was no explanation for it.

Hurrying back inside, the boys locked all the doors. Once they were in bed, Carson and Jeffery both heard the eerie sound of faint crying somewhere in the house beyond their closed bedroom door.

Neither of them went to investigate.

How did the ghost hunting kit get scattered far and wide? Was it done by ghostly hands, or human?

If human, then whose?

If ghosts did it, was it because the boys were getting too close to discovering them?

What made the crying sound in the night? Was it the wind? Or a sad spirit that didn't get to finish reading the ghost hunting book?

Zombie Portal

At school, twelve-year-old Jacob Taylor got the chance to choose a book to keep as his own. The one that caught his eye was "A Guide to Surviving a Zombie Attack."

Jacob picked up the book, carried it home, tucked himself into a corner of his living room couch, and read about how to trap zombies. He was happy to discover a bonus feature in the book that described how to detect ghosts, too. The book explained that the human body has an internal radar that indicates when there's something there, even though it might be invisible to the human eye. Jacob thought the information was in the book was kind of funny, that is, until he went to bed that night.

He was just dropping off to sleep when he heard a strange *thump*. His eyes flew open in alarm. *What was that?* Grabbing a flashlight, he shone it around his room, but saw nothing out of the ordinary.

After turning the light off, he heard another sound, a loud *clang* that sounded like a cast iron pan falling to the floor.

This time, Jacob jumped out of bed and headed for his door, ready to yank it open to see what might be out there. All of a sudden, his internal radar starting buzzing like crazy, and he thought, *There is something there.*

Using the information he'd recently read, he gathered his courage and asked aloud, "Why are you here? What is your purpose?"

While Jacob wondered if he was dealing with a ghost or some other paranormal situation, he noticed an unusual light glowing outside his bedroom window. Creeping across his room, he cautiously pulled back the curtain. What he saw was indescribable, but the closest he could think of was the gates of the Underworld opening outside his house. If that wasn't bad enough, he saw something that looked like a mottled hand reaching out through the gate.

Frightened nearly out of his wits, Jacob scrambled to grab anything to defend himself, and found his hand grasping the wooden hammer he'd made in shop class. As soon as his fingers tightened on the handle, he saw the devilish hand slide back inside the portal.

Slumping in relief, Jacob thought, *It's gone for good.*

Just then, he felt a presence behind him just as something grabbed his shoulder. Still holding onto his hammer, Jacob swung around to hit whatever had a grip on him, but there was nothing there. At least, nothing he could see.

"My internal radar went down a notch, then finally got back to normal," Jacob says.

But his ordeal is not over, because he sometimes dreams of the hellish portal opening and a fiendish hand sliding through. "It's been haunting me ever since," Jacob says.

Were the unexplained nighttime thumps from someone clumsily foraging for a midnight snack in the kitchen? Or were they the sounds of a devilish portal opening? Was Jacob dreaming? Or did his zombie/ghost book call forth an unearthly presence?

The Nurse

Nell Olsen often worked the night shift at the Gunnison Hospital while her husband and three girls slept. She didn't mind driving to her nursing job at 11:00 pm, because working the night schedule allowed her to spend time with her daughters when they got home from school.

Sometimes she'd tell them about strange lights she occasionally saw in the sky over Nine Mile Reservoir, a place she passed each night during her half hour drive to work. During a full moon, the round reflection stared out at Nell from the dark surface of still water like a white eye watching her pass. Moonless nights occasionally provided interesting light shows, with objects moving around the sky in unfamiliar ways. Nell declared they were like nothing she'd ever seen. They didn't behave like airplanes, satellites, or weather balloons. She had no explanation for some the erratic light behavior, but she didn't stop to try and figure it out. She simply drove on, did her job, and went home to her family mom.

One dark night, Nell passed the reservoir without incident. It was only when she drew closer to her destination that she noticed something out of the ordinary.

A narrow hamlet known as Christianburg extended along a road paralleling the highway for part of its length, yet was screened from view by a thick stand of trees. The strange thing is that after Nell passed the section of road that bordered Christainburg, she noticed a strange man sitting quietly in the passenger seat of her car. He had not been there when she left home, and she hadn't stopped along the way.

Initially startled, she felt no malice from him, so she kept on going. Neither one of them spoke as Nell drove the last couple of miles to the hospital and parked her car. As soon as she turned off the engine, she noticed that her passenger was no longer there. Glancing across the dark expanse of lawn with sharp shadows from the glare of bone-white street light, Nell couldn't see her mysterious passenger anywhere.

When Nell reported for duty, one of her coworkers said, "We just lost a patient from Christianburg."

A chill passed through Nell. "Male or female?"

With a puzzled frown, her fellow nurse answered, "Male. Why? Do you know him?"

"Maybe. Where is he?"

The nurse led Nell into the room where the body of the man who'd hitched a ride lay still in death.

She doesn't know why he hitched a ride with her. Perhaps he wanted to prepare her for the next ghostly incident in her life.

When Nell's husband passed away, her daughter Martha moved in to stay with her. One night the two of them were up late watching TV when they heard distinctive footfalls. It was the exact sound Nell's husband made whenever he got up in the night to go to the bathroom.

Nell didn't think anything of it until Martha asked, "Mom? Who's that?"

Nell said, "It's your father." Then she remembered that her husband was dead.

"Mom, it can't be."

Nell turned to her daughter, and with a gentle smile, replied, "Oh, but it can."

Were the things Nell saw a result of her being overly tired? Or did Nell have an affinity for seeing what other people didn't?

Were the strange lights in the sky some kind of natural occurrence? Secret government operations? Or the result of tired eyes?

What about the man in Nell's car? Was she imagining him? If so, why didn't she imagine other passengers on her many drives to work? Was the spirit of the man from Christianburg simply more used to riding in a car than floating, so he took advantage of a free ride?

The Ghost Who Watched Football

In 1960, Garth and Barbara Vest moved into a hundred year old house on a farm bordering Christianberg Road in Mayfield, Utah. The neighbors encouraged the Vest's to tear the modest adobe house down and build a new one. Even Garth thought it was a good idea to start fresh.

A Mayfield native, Garth was aware of the house's former occupants. The most famous was Old Lady Rass, so called because her husband was Rastus Anderson, making her Rastus's "old lady."

The old lady was notorious for throwing dead chickens at people riding by on their horses. More sobering than that is the fact that one of her sons was found hanging by the neck in one of the farm's outbuildings. General speculation was that she had done the hanging, but she was never brought to trial.

She was also known to brew beer in her basement, as witnessed by the local doctor who was cheerfully taken on a tour of her brewery during a home visit. Skimming a dead mouse off the top of a barrel of beer, Old Lady Rass dipped a generous portion for the good doctor to drink. Although he didn't want it, he drank it anyway, not daring to refuse.

"There was something funny about the whole family," Garth says, recalling an incident that involved his own grandfather. One of Old Lady Rass's sons courted a Mayfield girl, which concerned the young woman's parents to the point that they sent her away to live with relatives in order to keep him away. Garth's grandfather, the mail wagon driver, agreed to take her to the train station. Along the way, the jilted lover stood up from hiding in a clump of sagebrush along the road and shot at the wagon. Although the young lady was spared, Garth's grandfather got his arm shot off, but he lived to tell the tale.

In spite of its deranged history, something about the old house made Barbara insist on keeping it. In spite of the fact that it had broken windows and was used as a granary, generating a mouse infestation with a few skunks thrown in for variety, Barbara liked it well enough that she was willing to clean it up and move in.

The neighbors thought the Vest's were crazy to integrate the old structure with a fine, new addition. "We did more work that if we started with a new one," Barbara admits, "but I was happy."

"When we started living here, there was someone else living here," Garth says. It was someone they couldn't see. Not all of the Vest's five daughters and one son have felt the ghost. Some of those who did waited a long time to tell their parents, because they weren't sure they'd be believed.

There were times when Barbara was home alone that she was sure someone had come in the house, but she didn't find anyone there. "When I first realized that we were living in a haunted house, it was spooky," Barbara says. "After awhile, we got along just fine and it didn't really bother me anymore." After the Vest's put a lock on the front door so people couldn't just walk in, then Barbara knew that any presence she felt had to be Old Lady Rass.

The ghost was never belligerent or bothersome to Barbara, but it liked to tease the kids a little. Their son was especially bothered, which made him adopt the habit of sleeping with his head covered up. When he got married, he brought his wife home. She only slept one night in the old part of the house before refusing to sleep there again. "The ghost would never go in the new part," Garth says, "so we had to put beds down in the family room so they could sleep down there."

One day Garth came home from work early and snuck up on Barbara, who was busy putting clothes in the dryer. After giving her a playful pat on the rump, he says with a laugh, "It took me about an hour to get her out of the dryer."

Barbara often felt the ghost's presence while cleaning, as if it was curious about what she was doing. What was that big, roaring thing she pushed across the floor that ate up dirt like a hungry horse from a hay trough? What was that cylindrical thing in Barbara's hand that sounded like a hissing snake as it spewed bubbles on the bathtub surface that Barbara then wiped away with a cloth? What was that oddly shaped white barrel in the small back room that swirled water down a hole in the bottom before filling up again?

Finally, Barbara had enough. "I told her to leave me alone, I was too busy," Barbara said. After that, the ghost seemed to stay away from Barbara, but sought out Garth, especially when he sat in the old part of the house watching TV. "We have no idea if it was a man or woman," Garth explains. "It could be anyone, but we got to calling her Old Lady Rass,"

Another strong candidate for the ghost is a young man with the surname of Larsen. While his family lived in the house, he and a friend robbed a Wells Fargo coach. The rumor is that they buried their loot somewhere on the property. "We've had people in his family come down and ask to search for it," Garth says. "Just last summer they used high-powered metal detectors, and a rod that echoed off something buried in the ground. They showed me where it was. After they left, I got my son in law who lives across the road and told him all about it. We soon had a big hole out there, and it wasn't anything but a great big rock buried down in there."

While his children were growing up, Garth was not averse to telling them the stories of old coins that could be buried right beneath their feet. "If I needed a hole dug for a post, I'd tell my kids, 'That looks like a place they'd bury treasure.' The next day, there'd be a hole there."

Garth sees their unseen houseguest as a friendly old soul who would come in and sit by him while he watched football. "You can feel when someone sits beside you," Garth explains. "I never was bothered. I just figured she was an unloved old woman that liked to hang around. She didn't bother us."

The ghost bothered visitors, though. One day when the bishop visited the Vest's, the ghost came in and sat beside him. Without taking his eyes off his hosts, the bishop moved over to make room before turning to see that there was no one there. "You've never seen anyone with such a sick look on his face in your life," Garth says with a laugh.

Like the bishop, other people who laughed at their stories suddenly got a funny look on their faces while visiting. Then they started looking around, and pretty soon were ready to leave.

The Vest's have never seen the ghost, they just feel her. "Don't ask me why," Barbara says, "it's just a different feeling than we normally feel."

All of the Vest children accepted the reality of the ghost. One of their daughters decided to go to the cemetery and have Old Lady Rass's grave dedicated in the hope that the ghost would leave her alone. Their son also attempted to get the ghost to leave. "As soon as I found out about it, I invited her back in," Garth says. "She came back after he'd done that, but for a long time she just disappeared. She hasn't been around now for a long time. I've thought about it, and I think she she finally found contentment." He paused and looked around at the walls of old pioneer home. "We don't expect you to believe any of this, but we do."

Who is the spirit that haunted the Vest family for so many years? Was it the man who'd robbed the Wells Fargo shipment and buried his booty on the property? If so, does he remain behind to guard it? Or is it lonely Old Lady Rass, who was as confused in death as she'd seemed to be in life? Did she finally find peace beyond watching football with her benevolent host, and so moved on to another world?

Babysitter Ghost

When Yvonne moved into a 2-bedroom duplex with her two sons, Finn, twelve, and Indigo, five, it appeared to be empty.

But it wasn't.

After securing a part-time job at the elementary school, Yvonne also found a part-time evening librarian job to help make ends meet. Her sons could go to the library while she was working, or they could stay home with Finn in charge.

One night when she came home from work, Finn told Yvonne of an unusual experience. "Mom, I was just sitting on the couch watching TV when someone touched my shoulder," he said. "I thought it was Indigo, but then I saw him on the floor in front of me, so I hurried and turned around, but no one was there."

"Did either of you get hurt?" Yvonne asked.

"No. It was just weird."

"Well, then it must have been a kind spirit who came to babysit," Yvonne said. She kept her other thought to herself. Finn was the right age to generate Poltergeist activity, which is defined as unexplained events that might involve objects falling or flying across a room when no one is near them. It also manifests with mysterious loud noises. Sometimes a ghost or other supernatural being is blamed, and sometimes it is said to be the fault of cosmic connection to adolescent turmoil as they transition from children to adults.

Yvonne had to re-think her theory when the next incident involved her younger son. He called her at work, sobbing so hard he could barely speak, telling her that the rocking chair was rocking by itself. Then

Finn got on the phone and said, "It's true, Mom. I didn't do anything."

"Did someone open the door just before it happened?" Yvonne asked. "Was a window open, letting in a breeze?"

"No."

"Did anything else happen, like a fire? Were knives flying out of the drawers?"

"No. Just the chair rocking by itself."

"Well, don't you think it's kind of cool to have a ghost babysitter?"

Silence.

Yvonne glanced out the window at the crisp, autumn leaves scudding across the street. "You boys can walk to the library if you want to stay with me until I'm done."

After a moment of thought, Finn answered, "No, it's stopped now. I think we're good."

When Yvonne got home, the boys lingered in the front room with her, making excuses not to go into their room to go to bed. At last she stood up to walk with them into the dim room where the curtains were pulled tightly across their window. That's when she heard a loud "whoosh" that sounded just like a stage curtain falling closed. Startled, she turned to look at her boys, who stared back at her with wide eyes.

"What was that?" Yvonne asked.

The boys shrugged.

Yvonne went outside to see if she could find anything to explain the sound. There was nothing, only stars staring down at her from a velvety black sky. She shivered and went back inside to read to her boys until they fell asleep.

When she heard about a two-story rental house that had just come available, Yvonne jumped at the chance to get out of the apartment and move to a bigger place. It seems as if the ghost might have had the same idea.

Once they'd moved, a large scented candle tucked far back on the kitchen counter fell into the sink not once, but three times, over the course of a few days. Perfectly balanced, with a wide base, there was no logical reason for that to happen.

An even more frightening incident occurred on the day Yvonne was vacuuming. She and her sons were all startled to see the lights dim, then shocked when an electronic sizzle was followed by a short burst of flame shooting from the outlet sockets.

Fearful that faulty wiring might make the house burn down, Yvonne called an electrician. When he took the cover off the outlet, he examined the wiring and announced, "This fixture is fine." Yvonne looked over his shoulder, startled to see that there were no burn marks or singed odor coming from the outlet. The electrician discounted the dimming lights as well. "This type of light can't dim," he announced, bending over to re-affix the plate over the outlet. "They are either on or off. They don't have the capability of dimming."

"Well, then what happened?" Yvonne asked. "I'm not making this up. Both my boys saw it, too."

The electrician gathered up his tools and stood up. "There's only one explanation." He smiled. "You have a haunted house."

Did Yvonne really have a ghost that followed her from a duplex to a two-story house? Or, considering the mild events from the first residence to the more dangerous ones in the second, were there two different ghosts? Was it all caused by Yvonne's son, who had become a bona fide teenager by the time they moved to the larger house?

Since the electrician was a professional, did he know something she didn't when he pronounced the problem as a haunted house?

The Train House

The Victorian house on the west edge of town once served food to hungry passengers who went through the Manti, Utah train station. For decades, travelers hung their coats on the hooks inside the house's door, seated themselves at a long table, and enjoyed a fresh meal prepared in the big kitchen.

Since it was the station master's family residence, the house was not used as a hotel. Manti native Joel Harmon remembers charging two bits for picking up travelers and their luggage from the station house when he was just a boy and driving them to town in his horse-drawn wagon.

After a flood destroyed the rail line upriver, the train tracks were pulled up and the house was suddenly empty, making train whistles only the ghosts of memories.

After Lowell and Garna Clark bought the station master's house and moved their family in, they discovered that Archie Brugger's residence, three blocks east of theirs, was remarkably similar in construction. Archie told Garna that his house originally belonging to the station line master. The main difference between the two houses is that the Brugger's big center room is divided, while the station master's house is not, allowing more space for long tables and hungry travelers.

It appears that some of those travelers are still going through the old station house. At times, Garna was home alone when felt a presence, often accompanied by a flash of movement in her peripheral vision. When she looked, no one was there.

As the Clark's welcomed more children to their family, Garna could have sworn that while she was tending to her babies, an unseen someone walked past her shoulder on more than one occasion.

Garna's daughter, Sariah, was five years old when she woke up one night to see an unfamiliar lady standing in her doorway. Her first thought was, *Why is that lady staring at me?* In the way of children, Sariah closed her eyes to make the lady go away. When she opened them again, the lady was still there. *Close. Open.* Still there.

The lady made no threatening moves, so eventually Sariah's game of peek-a-boo sent her back to sleep. When she woke up in the morning, the lady was gone. Sariah told her parents about her visitor, but Garna and Lowell have no idea of the lady's identity.

When the Clark's relocated, they didn't sell their house. Instead, Paul and Denise Hagemeister moved in as caretakers. One day Denise was home alone cooking dinner. She looked high and low for her measuring spoons. After searching drawers, cupboards, the kitchen floor, and not finding them anywhere, she finally went to the store and bought another set.

When she got home, she opened a kitchen drawer and stared in disbelief at the missing measuring spoons spread out in a perfect fan shape on top of the regular silverware. She is certain they had not been there when she'd looked earlier, so where had they come from?

"Paul?" Denise walked to the bottom of the staircase, thinking her husband may have come home early. "Paul?"

No answer.

With a slight shiver, Denise got back to cooking. When Paul came through the front door, she asked if he'd stopped in while she was at the store and put the measuring spoons in the drawer. He hadn't.

Neither one of them have solved the measuring spoon mystery, or the one that happened when a visitor stayed overnight. Their guest made her bed in the morning with a quick flip of the covers up over the sheets.

When she returned later in the day, she found something odd on top of the bed. From the doorway, two small dark lumps sitting side by side on the bed looked like a pair of staring black eyes. Moving closer, the visitor was relieved to see that the objects were a pair of cufflinks. What they were doing there? They hadn't been there when she left her room. Had Denise or Paul put them there for some reason?

When she asked, neither of her hosts had any knowledge of the old-fashioned cufflinks. They'd never seen them before, and had no explanation for their mysterious appearance.

A flood damaged the Clark's house and created another mystery. When the insuring company water remediation specialist came to measure the damage to the walls, he pointed a device around the room to measure coolness or warmth. Cool showed up as blue in his viewfinder and meant wet walls. Red showed the warmth of dry walls.

As the insurance adjuster scanned the living room,

he suddenly said, "Whoa!"

"What?" Denise asked.

"Watch this." The man swung his indicator past a picture of Jesus hanging next to the fireplace. The walls radiated the distinct blue of water damage, while the picture of Jesus and the outline of wall around it showed as warm red.

"That must mean the picture isn't wet," Denise suggested.

"But watch this." The man turned his device to another picture. The walls were blue, and the picture showed as a lighter blue. "The wall temperature affects what is touching it," the man explained. "Since pictures are directly touching the wall, they should reflect the same temperature as the wall behind them." He swung his device back to the picture of Jesus and they both stared at the warm red rectangle encompassing the picture while the walls around it glowed blue.

The insurance adjuster had no explanation for the phenomenon.

Each summer, when the Clark's return to their house for a month-long family vacation, the Hagemeister's move in with Paul's parents. In 2015, there was a large family gathering at the train station home. With all their children and grandchildren filling up the rooms, Garna felt an unusual sense of happiness. The occasion seemed to reach beyond the joy of simply being with her family. It was as if the house itself were happy, too. This makes perfect sense when considering the home's original purpose.

Can a house really have a spirit? Or are the unexplained happenings the result of former diners returning? Did one particularly hungry spirit provide the measuring spoons? Was another one drawn to Garna's babies? Had the room where the cuff links appeared on a freshly made bed once belonged to the station master? Did the warm picture of Jesus mean that the house had good spirits in it? And when the Clark's gathered for a family celebration, did the spirits celebrate right along with them?

If you enjoyed "Who's Haunting You?" please let readers know on Amazon, Goodreads, or any other literary platform, because stories are magic…they never wear out.

AUTHOR BIOGRAPHY

Shirley Bahlmann is the author of numerous books ranging across a wide spectrum, from biography to fiction to how-to and how-not-to. "Who's Haunting You?" began when high school students told her stories of spooky things that happened to them. Then they told her of other people who'd encountered ghosts, and others, until it morphed into this book.

It seems there is a lot of morphing in her life.

Shirley is currently gathering more ghost stories for "Who's Haunting You 2?" Please send them to her via yoshirley@yahoo.com with "Ghost Story" in the subject line, or send them through her Facebook Page: https://www.facebook.com/shirleybahlmann

Feel free to haunt her website at www.shirleybahlmann.com

Thank You!